Game

Over

My Love for Hip Hop

Winter
RAMOS

LOVE & HIP HOP REALITY STAR

Life Changing Books
Published by Life Changing Books
P.O. Box 423 Brandywine, MD 20613

Library of Congress Cataloging-in-Publication Data;

www.lifechangingbooks.net
13 Digit: 978-1934230640
10 Digit: 1-934230642

Cover Photographer:
Seth Kushner Photography
Rashida Watler Super Femina Ent.

Acknowledgements

I want to thank my Lord and Savior for keeping me safe during my wild and crazy life. Thank You for taking me through the bad to eventually get to the great. I appreciate it with all of my heart.

To my mini me, I can't wait until you get here and meet us. Everyone has waited for you for so long. You are going to be a spoiled brat...so what you are your mother's child. World get ready for my mini me.

To my grandmother who gave up her life to make sure I had a great one, thank you. You always had my back and I thank you for everything. My step father, who I adore, I swear you are the best thing that has ever happened to me even though it took me some time to realize it. You are the best man ever and I'm sure they broke the mold when they made you. But thank God I found the closest thing. To my mother, who holds no bars, and who taught me to speak my mind and never back down. If you think I'm bad, Jackie is ten times worse.

To the love of my life and his three little bears, I love you guys and thank you for being so understanding when my life and schedule is so hectic. To my aunt, Leslie for teaching me no matter how much money he has, you better get your own. I know I've done things to disappoint you, but I got it right now and know everything you taught me stayed with me. Now, it's time to make you proud. Thanks for always letting me know there was more to life than just living in the projects.

To my best friend in the whole wide world and my favorite child. Keya you totally get me, and you gave me Na. I will forever owe you for that. Thank you for being the sister I never had. To Ebony and Raheem, my tag team. Thanks for always being real with me, and slapping me in the back of my head when I needed it most. Tina, Rosana and Renee thank you for being the older sisters I never had and all the "sit your ass down" comments when I was doing way too much. I can honestly say I have three older sisters that kick ass.

I also want to thank my Jamaican family for supporting me; Tracey, Raven, Sean, Ray, Lamar, Logan, Grandma, Toya, Brooklyn, Chrissy, Jeri, and Aliyah. To Indiya, my special child. I've seen you grow and happy to say, "You have finally gotten your life." A special shout out to Baby for being by my side and doing everything to help me through writing this book, filming, and having a baby. I love you guy!

Thanks to my fabulous publishing team for making my book a hit! Rockelle, Gilda, Simone, Kwiecia, Stephanie of Black Rose ENT and the entire roster of Life Changing Books authors, thanks for all the hard work and dedication. I know it's tough dealing with a firecracker like me, so thanks for the love and patience. Kellie, thanks for the hot book cover design. Thanks to my editor, Melody for the sharp eyes. A special thanks goes to Nicole Bey and Tiphani. I can't thank you enough for all the promotion on social media. Your contribution to this project is extremely appreciated.

To my publisher, Azarel- I know you're tired, but this next book is brewing. To everyone who has an opinion on my past just know this, it's not did I do it, but am I still doing it. Never judge others. And lastly…I'd like to thank Kiss for putting the battery in my back to write this book. If you ever need a loan, I got you! Ahhhhhhhh!

Muah!

Winter Ramos

Follow me on twitter @winterramos

WARNING

Imagine a sexy, A-list celebrity who's making millions and wooing you. He meets your homegirl, your mother, impresses your best friend, and tells you all the things you've always wanted to hear. *It's a dream come true.* Soon, he's spending all his free time with you...when he's not working or at the studio. He's at your beck and call, and you put the rest of the world on pause.

After a few months, you're telling everyone that you guys are a couple that is...until you're being dragged down the steps by your hair while you scream at the top of your lungs, "Noooooooo. Stop!Get off of me!!!!" The man who's supposed to be your protector is now kicking you like an animal in front of his friends, sending your body hurtling around the room. Now you're in a fetal position, crying out for help. People are watching but they stand by and do nothing. Months later, you're still in that relationship.

This is what I have seen in the crazy world called Hip Hop that took me from the Cypress Hill projects in Brooklyn to the offices of major record labels like Murder Inc., Def Jam and Ruff Ryder. And even into the arms of the CEO of the most successful, independent label out to date.

My name is Winter Ramos and I'm here to tell my story. Not out of spite nor animosity. But, because it needs to be told. It will not be easy for the many names that will get mentioned or the secrets that will be revealed; or even for the guy who has the smallest dick in the game...but I'm telling it anyway. It is my hope that both younger and older females who think being with a rapper or celebrity is all glitz and glam will learn from my mistakes and stop chasing that dream that eventually turns into a nightmare.

I hope those Hip Hop celebs mentioned who are married have pre-nups in place; you'll need them. To those who have rap careers hanging on by a string, get ready to be reborn, my story will boost your career. And to those rappers or industry execs who will flat out deny my story, get ready because you know I have proof.

Journal Entry - 2/20/12

Somebody slap me! Tell me today was all a dream. It was all a joke. Friends keep saying, "Winter, stop believing everything you read." But after Googling the effects of sexual intercourse, I froze. Someone wrote, "When a man ejaculates deep into a woman's vagina… It's unreasonable to think it will all drain out. What remains will be absorbed into the woman's body…and becomes an actual part of the woman with the potential to remain with her for the rest of her life. Thus a woman who has slept with several men, will carry a small part of each of her lovers with her forever."

Those words messed me up. Especially: "Forever." My mind raced. My heart thumped. I thought about all my sexual relationships with rappers, athletes and Hip Hop executives. All of their faces flashed before me: Dame Dash, Jadakiss, a Murder Inc. favorite and many more. I then thought about the tons of women they'd been with. The room seemed to spin at the thought of their sperm being re-absorbed as my very own cells. Geez…I quickly began researching online more and more, lasting late into the night with people commenting, saying the notion couldn't be true. But in my heart I now believed the bullshit that had been written and how each man I'd slept with had now become a part of me. I then started to think about their different personality traits and how each of

3

them had left me with something, or rubbed off on me in some way. I even thought about my first love, the man who'd obviously left me with major intuition, allowing me to recognize "Game" before it ever got too close. The notion that they each had contributed to my outlook on life made me think differently.

Undoubtedly some biologist somewhere will challenge me on this. But of course I'm not concerned with that. I actually believe this is true. And since it's my journal, my life, then who cares? My past is my past and cannot be erased. I've learned many things through my relationships, some I'm proud of and others I'm not. Maybe I'll tell my story soon, with hopes that women from everywhere will learn something from my experiences. Of course I'll be stepping on the toes of the men who'd rather keep our encounters a secret. But hey…Karma always comes knocking. I'm prepared. Let the games begin!

1   Groomed For The Game

Tear ducts...what the hell are those?

My mother, Jackie Natal, said I was born without them. Imagine bursting from your mother's womb unable to shed a tear. She said the doctor slapped my behind hard several times to make me cry but his borderline abuse resulted only in slight moans escaping my lips. A young mother at seventeen, she had no idea what to do with me. Like most kids in the projects, I didn't have a father so she had no support there. Well, I had one but he was more of a sperm donor than anything else. He saw me three days after I was born and a limited number of times since, ultimately becoming a ghost in my life. But that seemed to be the norm, none of my friends had fathers around.

My mother and I lived with my grandmother and two aunts in the Cypress Hill projects in Brooklyn, NY in a three bedroom apartment. Supposedly, from the first day my mother brought me home, I slept through the night. Most babies wake up crying, some at the top of their little lungs to let you know they're hungry. Not me. I guess my survival skills had already kicked in. My mother tells how she kept waking up and checking on me to make sure I was still breathing.

She often wondered why her child didn't cry every three to four hours in need of a bottle and went to my grandmother for advice. "That child isn't normal," my grandmother said. "What baby doesn't wake up for milk?" Night after night my mother continued to wake me up to feed me. But my grandmother, the matriarch of the family took a stand. She ordered my mother to stop feeding me. "I want to hear her cry," she demanded in her strong Puerto-Rican accent. "Stop feeding her until she cries for a bottle. Her lungs need to develop," she said. At first the story seemed unbelievable...but now I understand. I'm still searching for an answer about my lack of emotion at the age of thirty-three.

I've been told that I'm as cold as my name, 'Winter.' That comment should hurt...but it doesn't. It's who I am. I believe my kinks are innate while others say my experiences made me who I am today. I can say this: it wasn't the music industry that did it. I'd been that way all of my life. Maybe not having a father in the house affected me. Maybe I was born with a heart of steel. Or maybe growing up in a house full of strong women who told me early on that men weren't shit made an impression.

Some may think that four women living under the same roof in the hood would be chaotic...but we made it work. While that many females in one spot is usually a breeding ground for trouble, there wasn't a whole lot of bickering and cat fighting. It was just the opposite. My aunts, Leslie and Mickey, worked constantly, keeping pockets full of money while my mother worked, went to school, or just plain disappeared. My grandmother, Maria Natal, raised me like her own. I even started calling her 'mom' and my mother, 'Jackie.'

Still, I was spoiled rotten—like the baddest apple in the store. Jackie came over occasionally when I was a toddler and when she made an appearance, she always showered me with gifts. At the age of three I lived like a princess with a room full of Barbie dolls, the latest and most expensive clothes, the newest toys, and the best shoes—everything my heart desired.

Even though I grew up in the projects I never wanted for anything. Every month was like Christmas, and I'd developed this elite type mentality. Not many in my hood were doing it big like my family. It was all so unreal considering where we lived. But we were different. While all of our friends were black, in apartment 4D all the women were 100 percent Puerto-Rican. And unlike most people in the projects we were never on public assistance. There were no food stamps, no hands outs— none of that. All of the women in my household worked and made good money except for my grandmother who kept the ship afloat.

The combined paychecks allowed my family to spoil the only child in the house— me—even more. So living in the projects meant nothing to me. I never even realized there were bars on the window. My small but comfortable room was stocked with teddy bears, games and shelves filled with everything they had in the toy store. I had two televisions, one to watch and one for video games. I even had my own room, while everyone else in the apartment shared. Anything my heart desired, I got it.

One day, when my mother didn't meet my demands in our cramped kitchen things spiraled out of control. I was three years old and had asked her for something while my grandmother washed dishes nearby. Jackie's response was a word I rarely heard at that point: no. So I called her a bitch.

She flipped. "Go get a belt, Winter," she told me firmly.

I stormed off to get the belt, returning to the kitchen with a malicious smirk, and handed it to her boldly as if to say, "Now what?"

7

"You called me a bitch?" my mother angrily asked from the table, attempting to search my grandmother's eyes. My grandmother didn't turn around and kept washing dishes. My mother asked me again, "Winter, you called me a bitch?"

Eventually she got up and swung the belt aiming for my ass. Quickly, my rage erupted. "You bitch!" I called out, barely afraid.

My mother went wild and at the time I thought she would kill me. She kept swinging as I took refuge behind my grandmother's five foot frame causing water to splash and fly wildly across the tight kitchen. "You fuckin' bitch! You fuckin' bitch!" I repeated over and over again, screaming at the top of my lungs as I played defense across the kitchen floor.

My mother said I repeated those words at least ten times.

"Leave her alone," my grandmother finally shouted. Her robe and hands were soaked by now, and her eyes warned Jackie to stop.

"Yeah, Jackie, leave me alone," I interjected.

Of course that was the end. What my grandmother said was always boss. Jackie may have been my mother but it was what it was. The women in my life had created a monster and although I love her to death and am thankful for everything she taught me, Jackie wasn't around much. I had all the material things I needed…but something was still missing.

Maybe time with my mother?

Maybe discipline?

Maybe being assigned some chores for a change?

Not long after my third birthday my father resurfaced. We found out he'd turned into a junkie and was in jail. After he landed in Rikers Island, my mother got the call, the one that sent her running to his rescue with me in tow. My mother said she loved him and wanted me to have a father in my life, so we began visiting him at Rikers. They rekindled their relationship, he got clean and they moved to a fly place in Brooklyn leaving me with my grandmother, although I visited them occasionally.

At the time I didn't know my father had been labeled one of the biggest drug dealers in Brooklyn in the mid seventies. He was known as a flashy man with wads of cash in his pocket, and he possessed the finest clothes and best diamonds money could buy. But once my mother told him she was pregnant with me, their world changed. He stopped coming around and rumors surfaced that he'd been cheating on my mother.

Like the strong woman my mother was and is today, she left him—pregnant and all—telling him she didn't need a man if he couldn't treat her right. Even though he made an indescribable amount of cash in the street, there was no contact while my mother was pregnant. After my actual birth, he showed up three days later before disappearing again. That brief moment only brought my mother sorrow. Over the next three years, signs of my father's support were non-existent. He didn't supply any pampers, milk, childcare, clothing, or anything. But his lack of financial support didn't seem to bother my mother as much as the lack of interaction. She'd been taught that women should know how to take care of themselves and not rely on a man. And while she wanted me to have a positive male role model in my life, unfortunately, there were none around. My grandfather had moved away to San Francisco to work after twenty-one years of marriage and none of my aunts had positive relationships either.

Sadly, I never really connected with my biological father—physically or emotionally. I have a few, fuzzy memories of him. I remember going to my parents' apartment during one of those infrequent moments where they actually lived together and seeing some sort of needle and my mother shouting and screaming at the top of her lungs.

I knew something wasn't right about the needles so I told my grandmother what I saw when I returned home. Even at that young age, I knew how to manipulate. After that episode, my grandmother told Jackie, "I don't want her going with him again."

Eventually my mother left my father again and moved back in with us. She'd had enough of my father. But that's what I saw as a young child. Men always disappearing. The game apparently started early for me in life, one where I'd eventually fall into the arms of drug dealers, rappers, and athletes. But let's be clear. I was born ready for them.

Let's go!

2   Hood Life

May 1996. It was all a dream. Had to have been. At sixteen, I found myself strolling around the now infamous "JR Mafia House" on Atlantic and Saint James Place in the heart of Bed-Stuy, Brooklyn, NY where uppity people now call it, Clinton Hill. Back then it was simply a bright red house in the hood where fun times were had and memories were made with some of Hip Hops' greatest.

Owned by three members of Junior Mafia and their families, the house was the place where rising stars like Biggie, Lil Kim, Faith Evans, Foxy Brown and Lil Cease hung out. Biggie had signed JM to his label right after his debut album, "Ready to Die," started to take off. Being around the house didn't really seem like a big deal for me, a thin Puerto-Rican long-haired chick who should've seemed out of place, yet their family treated me like I belonged. There were no security guards, big bags of money, or plastic surgeries going on. Biggie was the only one who'd blown up slightly, and the others were still striving for even a little taste of success. Everyone was on the come-up—even the house, which desperately needed repairs.

Often, the guys would hang out on the stoop, spitting

raps and kickin' it. That world felt like home to me. Me and my friends would also sit outside on the stoop, just as they did, or head over to Franklin Ave in the heart of Bed-Stuy until late in the night. But the guys in the Junior Mafia house were older cats—more mature, with more experience, and dreams of becoming household names.

Most people in Brooklyn recognized the members of Junior Mafia when they saw them, but only a few members had the money to match their celebrity status. Most were broke, on the grind, and working hard at spreading their music around the world.

They were out on the block day after day, and, since they were unknown, they were doing what all people in New York know how to do: survive, and hustle—hustle hard. I'd gotten caught up with one of the hardest working guys in the house, Nino Brown. He was my connection to the group and gave me an entrée into their world and my first taste of the music industry. I liked Nino a lot, even adored him slightly, even if I had to pretend that he didn't have bad, scaly skin and a wack sex game. It was his funny personality that kept me coming around. He had that spontaneous, anything goes type spirit that reminded me of the dudes I hung out with in my hood. Often, I splurged on Nino, buying him clothes and kicks since his pockets were always flat. But I wasn't using my money; it was Smiley's, a dude from the streets that I'd met a few months prior to hooking up with Nino, who ironically had my heart even in his constant absence.

Although Nino was a part of Junior Mafia, had a record deal and a hot song playing on the radio nonstop, he had absolutely no money. I'm not sure what the deal was financially between him and Biggie. All I knew was Nino was still living at home with his mom and *never* had any money, so I'd formed an opinion early on that while being with a rapper gave me proximity to glitz and fame, there was no paper to take care of my wants.

It was cool. I wasn't out for Nino's money. Smiley, my other boy toy, had plenty. Smiley was nine years my senior at twenty-five years old. He seemed so much more mature and experienced than me and introduced me to a pampered lifestyle, kept tons of money in my pocket and was the first man to make me feel like a woman. In a way, he took the place of my father, who'd never been present in my life. Smiley took care of me and would always say, "I'm your daddy now." Combined with his curly hair and West Indian features, those words made me fall even harder for him.

Smiley drove a drop top BMW and had a different Rolex for every day of the week, something I never saw with the guys my age. At first, I wasn't quite sure what his grind was. But whatever it was, it allowed him to keep thousands of dollars in his pocket at any given time, put us up in expensive hotel rooms in the heart of Manhattan, and fund extravagant trips out of town. Other girls my age didn't have those opportunities. We went on luxurious shopping sprees where he would buy me "Gator Boots for Girls" as Biggie would say and all the hot shit at the time: Moschino, MCM bags, fresh kicks and jewels. The experience amazed me. I had always felt loved...but now I had gained a sense of entitlement and expected Smiley to step up to the plate.

Smiley became my lover, father, mother and friend.

He'd do spontaneous things like show up at my high school unexpectedly and drive me all around the city giving me whatever I wanted. Once he picked me and a few of my good friends up, Nikeya and Mijiza after school for what we thought would be a normal day. We ended up hanging out in Manhattan for a day of fun, then stopping by a liquor store just before ending up in a movie theater with bottles of Cristal.

As time went on, our relationship grew stronger and I found myself staying away from home more and more. My mother had fallen in love and moved to the Poconos with my step-father by then leaving me to live with my grandmother who I adored. She was the coolest in my eyes and allowed me to have free reign. Her only rule was that I continued to do well in school. My grades were above average and my education at Clara Barton High School came easy to me, so there was no sweat with that, although my sarcastic mouth continued to cause trouble for me.

It helped that my grandmother trusted and liked Smiley a lot, which made life easier when I had to miss a few days of school to roll with him out of town. This might have been unheard of for most young girls, but my grandmother trusted whatever story I fed her. It was "our" way of life. Besides I'd told her and my mother that Smiley was a college student. Neither had any idea that he was a major drug dealer who bedded me every other weekend at extravagant hotels in different cities. For me, this was the life. Being a teenager from the hood and spending nights out pretending to be rich fueled me. Little did I know our secret would soon back fire.

Being young and dumb, I assumed Smiley's sex was the bomb. Not because he made my toes curl but because our sensual loving sessions would start and end with bottles of Cristal followed by room service with chocolate covered strawberries, fruit platters, and fancy desserts. Clueless and inexperienced, I didn't know back then how to satisfy a man. Smiley called himself schooling me, but now in hindsight I realize his loving scored low on my scale. Maybe that's why he always tried to convince me to give him head, which I thought was gross.

In my usual sarcastic tone, I'd often tell him, "That's for them Harlem chicks."

He'd laugh it off and say, "Oh, you will eventually Winter."

Even though Smiley wasn't a stallion in bed, he still had my mind. Wherever he told me to go, I went. Whenever he called, I came. This man controlled me like a puppet even from out of town. When he said he wanted to teach me how to drive I showed up to meet him. That day sticks in my mind even now. Smiley pulled up to the lot and said, "Winter, I told you if you learned to drive my car, I'd buy you your own as soon as we get you a license. Well, we getting you a car, baby."

I just knew I was the Queen of Sheba and the richest chick in the hood. That was my mentality, always happy to get more, adding to my pot. We went to the car dealer and looked at Mercedes-Benzes, Land Cruisers and everything else that was hot at that time. My face beamed with excitement when Smiley stopped in front of a .325 convertible BMW and grinned my way. All I had to do was learn to drive. Suddenly an Acura pulled up to the curb and screeched to a stop, startling us both. The driver's door opened and a stylish woman in her twenties hopped out enraged.

Immediately, she stepped up on the curb, walked onto the lot and began spazzing on Smiley. He kept his normal, cool disposition and acted like everything was okay. The only thing he said was, "Get back in your car and go home." Apparently she was his *other* chick, something he'd neglected to tell me. She appeared to be older than me, richer than me and obviously more intense. He was definitely taking good care of her from the look of her jewels and the fur coat she rocked. I had lots of mouth, always bragging about my fighting skills, but I said nothing as they argued. I realized I'd been played.

Smiley had been running game on me. We'd been spending every other weekend together, so it never occurred to me that he had another chick. I looked the woman up and down while her head bobbed back and forth. *Oh, so this is how real women get down?* I thought to myself. She knew how to get more from him than weekend trips. I knew I had to step up my game and ask for more if Smiley stayed in my

15

life. Unfortunately for her, while in the middle of her rant, Smiley punched the girl in her mouth, harder than he would've hit a three-hundred pound man. I'd never seen him do that before—not to me, not any one. I stood on the pavement dumbfounded. After he struck her, he warned what would happen if she didn't carry her ass home. With tears in her eyes and blood dripping from her mouth, she did exactly as she was told.

Strangely, I chose to stay with Smiley after that. I was young and in love with him in spite of discovering that he'd cheated on me and would actually hit a woman. The punch bothered me more than the cheating. Memories of my younger years were filled with infidelities from the significant others of all of the women in my house. My Aunt Mickey managed to have a long lasting relationship, but her man never married her and years later she found out he had been screwing other chicks the whole time they were together. Then there was my Aunt Leslie's husband who frequently took her hard-earned money for himself and treated her like she was garbage. He'd even had a baby on her during their relationship. And even though I wasn't born when my father cheated on my mother with another woman the story still sticks with me. I expected men to cheat so his having another woman didn't upset me.

Smiley promised never to lay a hand on me, and I believed him. I trusted him and he was my everything. Smiley had planted the seed that he was a *man* while everyone else I'd dated prior was a boy. He played on the fact that my mom and stepfather were far away, my real father was nonexistent, and that he was the one who'd always take care of me. His words about me not having a father around hit home-hard. For some strange reason, my love for him grew stronger and I wanted to spend the rest of my life with him. Instead, he cheated even more as months passed.

I was getting played but instead of getting even I decided to stay quiet and keep enjoying the lifestyle to which I had become accustomed. Besides, Smiley's infidelity gave me the opportunity to chill with Nino even more. In contrast to the fabulous excursions and the wining and dining with Smiley, Nino and I would have sex on a raggedy bed and eat beef and broccoli from the Chinese spot—followed by blunts. More and more people began frequenting the house the more popular Nino and Junior Mafia became. Soon they even had bodyguards. As their money increased so did Nino's ego. Neither meant much to me because I had everything I needed. While Lil Kim and Junior Mafia rapped about fly gear and jewelry, I lived that lifestyle compliments of Smiley's money. Still, Nino's life as a rapper began to include me less and less.

In July of '96 Smiley told me he was taking me to Vegas. I was super excited. I'd never been to Vegas before and couldn't wait. It was going to be one of the most exciting moments of my life. I saw myself tearing the strip down, splurging on any and everything Smiley's money could buy. It was going to be wild. On the day we were to leave, I went shopping to prepare for the trip and bragged to my home girls while waiting for Smiley to pick me up. My bags were packed and my anticipation was at a crazy level. When the call finally came, it wasn't the one I'd expected.

"Smiley's dead," Troy, his best friend told me. The words didn't register at first. I thought it was a joke. It had to be. There was no way that could be true. Smiley meant far too much to me to be gone. Besides, I'd just seen him earlier. How could he be gone so quick? But despite my denial, it really was true. The streets had taken Smiley, my daddy, my everything.

Earlier that day, Smiley decided to stop at the pager store to get a new beeper. After leaving the shop and crossing the street to his car, a fifteen year old boy ran up on him, robbing and shooting him. He died instantly in front of the Coliseum Mall, I'd never experienced that kind of heartbreak. I'd never felt a loss like that before. His death shook me…badly…to the core. My security blanket was gone and no one could console me: not my grandmother, my mother, nor my stepfather. Smiley became another man missing from my life. What hurt me even more was the way he died. To picture him on the street, dead, and murdered so brutally was unbearable. For months, his shooting occupied my nightmares.

Smiley's death left me depressed. He was my better half. He was the first man I truly loved. Without him, I felt dead inside. The world seemed dark and lonely. No matter how much I cried, the pain wouldn't stop. It wouldn't even ease up. I wanted to die at times. For months I rarely left the house except to go to school. My family was shocked to see my tears. They never thought I would cry over a man. Maybe even I'd begun to believe what people said about me: that I had a heart of stone and insides of steel. My outpouring of emotion confirmed to everyone what Smiley really meant to me.

The downside of my mother finding out about my feelings for Smiley was that she learned about all the trips I'd taken with him and that he was significantly older than I originally portrayed. While I sobbed, somehow she'd found all my receipts from shopping and traveling with Smiley. She also found out he was a drug dealer. She expressed her thoughts letting me know my life would change drastically. "The extravagant gifts are over," she warned. "And you're going to have to get a good job to keep up that lifestyle."

But I felt grown and had the mentality nothing could be done to me. No punishment would stick. How can you punish a jetsetter? She didn't. She took me to Disney World to grieve instead. As time moved on, I called my own shots just as Smiley had taught me and how my family allowed me to.

I turned to Nino for comfort and reconnected with him during the early months of '97'. I also spent time with my step-father who, I'd just discovered, really wasn't out to hurt me and my mom. I realized around that time that he really cared. He was an easy-going man who owned a camera shop in Park Slope although he and my mother still lived in the Poconos. He told me not to worry, he was there for me. He also told me to always work hard for myself. I weathered the storm a little better after that, but little did I know, Nino's entire world would turn black too. Not just his world, the entire world of Hip Hop.

Biggie was shot and killed out of the blue.

Just like the day of Smiley's death, that day in March of '97 will forever be branded in my memory. Sitting in the Junior Mafia house, we all thought the news coming out of L.A. wasn't true. We refused to believe it. But eventually, just like the rest of the world, we all had to accept that Biggie was gone.

Nino was crushed about Biggie's death. All of the Junior Mafia crew was. The laughter and smiles that had once filled the house on Atlantic and St. James ceased. The good times seemed to have stopped the day Biggie died, and it was like the air had been let out of everyone. I remembered Big as being funny, cracking jokes and having that personality that shined. Biggie was their heart. He was the one who was going to make all their dreams come true and change their lives. Without him, Junior Mafia couldn't function.

To help Nino through his loss, I went back to the Junior Mafia house often. During that time, obviously the mood wasn't the same anymore. The house was always somber and sad. Grown men were crying. Instead of a party like before, it now always seemed like a funeral. Without Biggie's jokes and larger than life presence, the house seemed empty no matter how many people were there. Even visits from Puffy and Mase, another up-and-coming rapper at the time who dropped by regularly to show support, couldn't change it. The loss was so huge for Nino that he just didn't have it in him to try and make our relationship work. It died just like the two people who had meant the most to us.

But Smiley left me with a level of maturity and savvy that would become dangerous in years to come. I now had an even harder heart than before covered by armor no man could break. Thanks to Smiley, and all of his crafty dealings I'd learned to manipulate my way through life through the eyes of a man.

3   Schemin'

All I did was party and bullshit around. That's one of the perks of living in the Big Apple. But this particular night set the rest of my life in motion. It was still 1997 when I entered a lounge on 44th street in Manhattan adjacent to Daddy's House, Puffy's studio. A party was being thrown by Sean Combs, P. Diddy or Puff Daddy, as he was called back then. That was before he started changing his name to something new every other week. Dressed in a black Versace dress with spaghetti straps that held my growing figure in place, I waltzed inside like I owned the place. At seventeen my curves weren't the way I wanted them, but they did the job for someone my age. My hair had just been shaved in the back and cut into a sassy bob that matched my feisty attitude and I had a fresh French manicure.

The party was one of many types that Puffy, or the preferred name now Diddy, would later grow a reputation for throwing. Lots of NY celebrities were in attendance. Some were big and well known like Mary J Blige, who with her dark shades and hood swagger seemed like she was still just another girl from the Slow Bomb Projects in Yonkers. Others

21

were just beginning to make a real splash like Faith Evans and Lil Kim. Even though neither of them remembered me from the JR Mafia House, at least they didn't display any diva egos…at least none that I could see. Everyone seemed like family, although not everyone was signed to Bad Boy. There weren't any overbearing bodyguards and everyone was chillin' out and mingling. Nino wasn't there and I didn't ask about his whereabouts. We'd had our time together, and because of him my love for Hip Hop was born. I thank him for that but my taste in men had changed. I now wanted a baller.

The party was the perfect atmosphere for catching a man with deep pockets. It wasn't stuffy or bougie but more like ghetto fabulous. The broads weren't stuck up or fighting for attention like groupies. There didn't seem to be any jealousy. Everyone was cool and my homegirls: Nikeya, Ayanna and Mijiza and I felt like we were a part of something big. Thick as thieves, we had gone to crazy measures getting everyone out the house. Luckily Mijiza and I were able to pull a fast one and sneak Nikeya and Ayanna out of the house. Mijiza at seventeen already had a baby so like me, we didn't have to answer too many questions about where we were going. On the other hand Ayanna, who'd been my girl since junior high never really went out too much. Her parents were strict so actually getting out for the night had us pumped.

It was difficult for me to wrap my mind around that moment. I was fresh out of high school and hadn't seen too much of the flashy side of the music industry. Up-and-coming hungry rappers from the streets were all I'd rubbed shoulders with at that point. And since Smiley's death I somehow found hustlers more and more attractive; attempting to replace the lavish gifts Smiley had thrown my way. I missed that life, and Puffy's event attracted the type of guys I yearned for.

Nino hadn't taken me to any music industry events that were even close to being as lavish. It was amazing. I had been given a chance to be close to celebrities even though I wasn't one of them. The shit was one of the most incredible feelings of my life. That life changing moment came when a tall, slim cat approached me. His lips were full and thick. His smile had a sort of cockiness to it. His swag was one of the most confident I'd ever seen. He was kind of cute, although many people beg to differ. He introduced himself to me as Jay-Z. The name wasn't familiar at the time. I didn't know he was the cat who'd just released what is now considered a Hip Hop classic, the album Reasonable Doubt. At that moment, he was basically in the same position as Faith and Lil Kim. He was a new artist trying to make a come up, and I hadn't heard of him.

After he introduced himself, we made small talk for a moment and exchanged numbers. And that was that. After several hours of mingling and enjoying myself, my homegirls and I headed home. The very next night, I basically repeated the previous night: more parties, more fun. That's New York night life or Vampire Life as some cats like to call it nowadays—work and hustle all day, party all night, especially during the summer.

On this particular summer night, I wasn't by myself. I had a couple of my babes from Queens with me: Renee, Rosana and Tina. They were older but crazy and wild like me—products of the hood. They repped Queens *hard* everywhere they went and always made for good entertainment. They knew how to make me laugh. They always made the party even more enjoyable.

Dudes were all over the spot. I mean, there were more thugs up in the place than I'd seen in a while. They outnumbered the females at least 5 to 1. Some of them were hot, others weren't. And believe me, my homegirls spent the entire night snapping on the ones that weren't, embarrassing them to the fullest, and doing things like exposing the girls with the fake bags. Like I said, the people I hung out with were really wild. That's how we grew up; down for whatever, always keeping it real. They were firecrackers just like me.

Eventually, a dude walked up to me. Little did I know that meeting him would be a pivotal moment in my life. The guy was tall, muscular and stocky, with a medium brown complexion and shaved head. His teeth were pearly white and unusually straight as if they'd been lined up with a ruler. He was sexy yet cocky, but there was still something different about the way he carried himself. With his white-Tee and iced out watch, he had that rugged New York swagger. Everything he had on attracted me even though it was nothing fancy, maybe because he rocked it in a different way. The shit was sexy.

He introduced himself to me and we spoke for a while. Within minutes, he was making me blush. That was rare. I mean, the dude was so slick with his words he had me visualizing us together. I liked him right off. But then just as quickly as he'd approached me and started a conversation, he handed me a business card and said he had to go. That was definitely a first. No man had ever given me a business card before, but of course my expression didn't show that. I simply smiled. Watching him walk away, I stuck the card in my purse.

The very next day I called the number on the card. The phone was answered by a secretary. I asked for Dame Dash, the name on the card. Quickly, the secretary put me on hold. As I waited, a song played, one that sounded familiar. I'd been hearing it in the streets but didn't know who the artist was. I looked at his card unsure of how he was affiliated in the music industry. Damon eventually answered. We only spoke for a moment. He said he was in the middle of business but assured me he wanted us to talk. I hung up thinking, 'whatever!' Then I got my detective game on.

It was obvious Mr. Damon Dash had something going on so I decided to do some research. I didn't want to go in blind if I didn't have to. Since this was the late 90's, the internet was still in its infant stages and Google nor I-phones existed, so I had to investigate the old fashioned way...ask around my hood and get my ear to the streets—fast.

The streets always talk, especially if the subject was about one of their own. Come to find out, Mr. Dash was definitely one of their own. Not only him, but Jay-Z, too. Dame was from Harlem and Jay was from Brooklyn. Both had been well known hustlas in the streets but decided to partner up and start a record label called Roc-A-Fella Records. At that time, the label's debut album Reasonable Doubt was making noise in the industry. Jay, as an artist, was making such an impact and he'd even appeared on a few tracks with Biggie. The Roc-A-Fella movement was beginning to take shape.

As the summer moved on, Dame and I went out a number of times and got to know each other. He figured out I wasn't flipping like most females if he didn't call often or when he said he would call. Groupie characteristics just weren't in my blood. Besides, it was difficult for us to hook up because he was so damn busy. Since Roc-A-Fella was just starting, he was heavily involved in promoting and taking the company to the next level. That was a full time job. So we got together when we could. I remember the first time seeing Jay at the office. It was awkward in the beginning since I'd never told Dame that I met Jay first and that we'd exchanged numbers. I showed up with a blank look on my face hoping Jay wouldn't blast on me, telling the real story. He didn't. Jay's reaction was just as bland as mine and reeked slickness. "Oh, you look familiar," he said to me. I smiled and we both left it alone from there. Yet in the back of my head my thoughts spiraled and I'd joke with my girls later in life:

Damn, I chose the wrong nigga. Honestly, I'll admit now that I'm older, although Dame was fly, Jay's swagger was a little louder, a little more sexy. It's just that I knew early in life from my experiences with Nino's crew that the CEO's and executives made the real money as opposed to the rappers and singers. Who would've known Jay-Z would turn out to be King. I could've been "King Bey" watching the throne, giving birth to the golden child. Not! Instead, I got Mr. Dash.

Even though no one knows where he is now, back then Dame was getting money—period. He took me places that Smiley hadn't, like on the set of videos where he and Jay would pop bottles of champagne on boats, have the flyest chicks and attract the jetsetters in the industry. We ate in expensive restaurants with names I couldn't pronounce, had the best seats at the hottest shows, and always got special treatment at clubs like the Latin Quarters where we were surrounded by security. Jay hosted the party while Dame handled business as usual. I felt like a boss just standing next to him. Dame captivated me with his business moves. He opened up my eyes to new places and another world.

I'd heard a lot in the streets about how Dame was arrogant and would get in your shit if you got out of line. But with me. I never saw that side of him early on. I definitely never saw him get that way with Jay. Understand that he would let you know he was in charge and that you needed to follow orders but I think he got a bad rap for his attitude. There were rumors of him being flashy and wild but that didn't happen much around me. That was for show: the Dame that surfaced in public, to dance in front of the camera or make a scene for reporters. The Dame I knew had his mind on building an empire, blowing up Jay-Z. He was about that cash, which he ran through like water, splurging on anything out of the ordinary, keeping wads of money in his pocket and funding his penthouse in some high rise in Fort Lee, New Jersey. The entire place was laced with mirrors, which was the shit back then. He even had a personal chef. The posh way he lived was *crazy*! It was the type of shit I'd only seen on television. But what really bugged me out was the very first whip I saw him push. In '97, the hottest guys in the streets were riding Benzes and Beamers. But Dame took it to the next level. He swooped me up one day in a lavender four-door Bentley. That blew my young mind! I couldn't relate. And as much as Smiley had taught me not to be a groupie—I was way too impressed. No one in the streets was doing it like that. To top it off, Jay pulled up right behind him in a blue Bentley coupe. Boss!

I was quickly falling for Dame, but I wasn't in love with him but with his swag and the way he lived so fabulously. My heart never allowed me to love a man since Smiley's death. My relationships were about sex only, which I reserved for the select few—those who were financially well off. Dame had the money, he just sucked in the bedroom. I do literally mean sucked. He got off on licking me like a cat licks its newborn kittens. The memory of his tongue slurping in my ear, filling it with saliva still haunts me now. All that nasty wetness made the sex horrible. Still, Dame had that power, paper and the ability to show me things I'd never seen before.

So my summer turned into a fairy tale. I was fresh up out the projects but getting a chance to travel frequently. But most importantly, it felt like I was a part of something, something huge. Roc-A-Fella was growing and I was getting a chance to see it up close and personal. There was nothing like it. It also felt great to see black men getting money and finding success outside of the dope game. That was a huge reality check for me. Since most of the men I'd been around before Dame were heavy in the streets, my mind was conditioned to believe drugs and the streets were all there was for them. I'd even found myself asking Dame if the cars and clothes were *all* coming from music. "Yes," he'd answer irritated with my questioning. It was hard to believe. I was still too young back then to understand just how businesses were built. Dame was showing me the possibilities of being a business owner first hand.

During our time together, although he gave me as much time as he could, he was always on the phone, usually about business. There were discussions with his associates about Roc-A-Fella's next step, such as other artists, movies, endorsements, etc, etc. Even back then, he wasn't content with just owning a label. He wanted a conglomerate and he was relentless at achieving it.

Most women would have been bored to death with such an ambitious man, especially those as young as I was. But real talk: it all intrigued me. Watching a powerful man make moves, always having dreams, keeping focused on his vision and never giving up in a cold industry. I loved watching, learning, and being in the mix. I felt like he was a teacher and me, the student. It was because of him, my determination multiplied. His work ethic had rubbed off on me although at the time I didn't know it. I realize now, he was helping me grow up. Sometimes, I'd get upset since he ate, slept, and drank Roc-A-Fella. With him, it was Roc-A-Fella first and everything else second, including me. Well, with the exception of his first born who was roughly six years old at the time. Seeing him in father mode did something to my insides. It made me wonder why my father was never as involved with me as Dame was with his son, which made me think back to my infrequent times with my biological father.

Riding in his car, I felt empty inside. My long, pig tails swung as I kept my face turned to the window. As usual there wasn't much conversation. There was nothing to talk about. It was like being with a stranger, the strangers my grandmother warned me about, yet this was my biological father. At nine, I had no choice but to go with him since that's what my mother had ordered. I talked shit in my head as we drove knowing that if my maternal grandmother found out she'd go nuts on everyone. The last time I had been in my father's presence was about three years prior. It didn't turn out too good and after that my grandmother forbade me to go around him ever again. She had no idea my mother allowed him to pick me up.

Although my facial features resembled his, we had nothing more in common. Even at that young age, I understood the rumors about the heroin and his drug usage. I understood some of the stories I'd overheard about him cheating on my mother when she was pregnant with me. I understood the talk about him being in and out of jail. It scared me to the core. Even though I grew up seeing people in the neighborhood using drugs, to know that your own father was one of them did something to my insides. I rode in silence hoping he'd at least drop me off at his mother's house like he always did, the few times he picked me up since him and my mother had split for the last time. At least there I would be safe.

It didn't take long to arrive at his mother's house, which was also in Brooklyn. It was the only place he knew to take me, getting me off of his hands. A smile slipped from the side of my mouth as soon as the car door opened. It was an opportunity to both get away from my father, yet also play with my many cousins whom my paternal grandmother took care of.

As soon as I stepped inside, the hugs and kisses flew from my grandmother and some cousins too. I hadn't seen them since the last infrequent visit but nothing had changed. The stares began from a few. They were the only family in my age group, but they were way different from me, which made me the black sheep at my paternal grandmother's house. I'm certain they hated the fact that our grandmother, their caregiver, catered to me when I showed up. It was clear that even without a father in my life, my status differed from theirs.

With so many deaths and suffrage on their side of the family along with seeing my father in and out of prison, it was abnormal to me. Life at their house felt like everyone was always grieving, so much turmoil, so much drug use— the exact opposite of my household with my maternal grand-mother, mother and aunts. Still in all I commenced to play-ing, allowing just enough time for my father to disappear again; something he'd do for years to come.

In hindsight, I can only compliment Damon on his par-enting skills. He showed me that all men didn't just shoot during sex, become a donor, and roll out. However, things were just about to heat up in our relationship. Summer ended and it was time to get focused on my first year of college. Of course, I hated to leave behind the limelight but I'd promised my grandmother and Aunt Leslie I'd go to Delaware State to make the family proud. My aunt was big on education and spoke about the importance a lot. I knew I needed to make them all proud, especially my mother.

Just like most parents, my mother had big dreams be-fore she had me. They didn't quite work out after giving birth to me. So she worked for years to bring money into our household; especially since there were no men to take care of the women in my family. She eventually went to school to be a phlebotomist. It wasn't what she wanted but she was forced to learn that life is rarely about what you want to do. It's about what you *got* to do. She didn't want me to have to set-tle and she knew a college education would be the best way for me to follow my dreams. What she didn't know, though, was my dreams were revolving around Hip Hop and the en-tertainment industry. I didn't know quite where I would fit in. Obviously, I couldn't rap or sing. But something inside me had me feeling the industry was where I belonged.

My mother would always beat my head in with how important it was for a Puerto Rican woman to get an educa-tion and take care of herself. She'd always preached about

Puerto Rican women taking advantage of every opportunity afforded them. I listened and started my first semester. But little did she know her advice had backfired. Yes, I was going to get an education and take advantage of opportunity, but quite differently than she anticipated. I would attend classes at Delaware State but would also attend Hip Hop University, where various rappers and moguls would be my professors. I had gotten infatuated with Hip Hop and planned to graduate at the top of my class.

4 Game 101

After being around Dame and his glamorous lifestyle for an entire summer, my sense of entitlement had increased. It was bad enough that I'd been spoiled by my mother's family my entire life, but now I felt as if I deserved the best— nothing less. The gifts Dame showered me with and the "benefits package" that came along with being around him made me want more.

I expected it.

Craved it.

Was willing to do whatever to get it.

In August '97 one of my closest friends, Nikeya, and I moved into our dorm at Delaware State. By then my chest was out and my hips had spread slightly. The "I'm real grown" attitude had taken on a life of its own. Since I'd told my mother that I didn't need anyone to take me to college, I opted to roll with Nikeya and her father who had a huge truck full of our stuff. After spending time away from home and living like my own boss, I figured checking myself into college was only appropriate. Besides, my mother was on vacation in Orlando.

What should've been an exciting time turned sour. My first foot into the dormitory put one of my famous frowns on my face. The décor wasn't at all what I had expected. Where was the luxury? It was small and crowded. There were girls everywhere, some of them already eyeballing me. Probably trying to figure out my ethnicity. I got that reaction a lot until people heard me speak. I wasn't tripping. With Hispanic features and straight hair most people assumed I was mixed until I opened my mouth. Then they wondered about me even more.

While headed to our room, Nikeya and I noticed the bathrooms. The showers and toilet stalls were lined up side by side with no privacy. I could actually smell piss. My stomach turned. When we finally reached our room and opened the door, the inside was tiny as a damn jail cell. How did they expect two people to live in there without crawling over each other like ants? The closets were tiny so I didn't have any room for most of my clothes and shoes, some of which still had the tags on them. I also noticed there wasn't a bathroom or shower in the room. That meant I would have to share the shower with a bunch of other broads. That wasn't sanitary in my book.

Immediately, I felt like a downgrade had taken place. I'd gone from chilling with Dame in his plush spot and lavish hotel rooms to *this*. In all actuality, I was there for an education. Living conditions shouldn't have mattered. I was getting the opportunity to go to college. I should've been grateful but I didn't see it that way back then. I'd grown used to being catered to. I'd grown used to being pampered. At that moment, I knew dorm life wouldn't work for long.

The first couple of weeks went by quickly. I was homesick and missed Dame. The dudes at the school were alright but not my type. They seemed cheesy. Call me stuck up, but I really didn't want them speaking to me. They tried but their game just seemed lame to me. I wasn't searching for a man but life sometimes has a way of making its own rules. What's meant to be is meant to be.

One day Nikeya and I were in the cafeteria, sitting at the table in the dining hall with me dressed in expensive gear. I was rocking a Movado watch adorned with a blinged out face, which was unusual for the average college student. But then again, nothing about me screamed normal. It seemed like everyone had a compliment about me, my hair, the way I talked, walked, or how I dressed. One dude named Jonathan tried to use his compliment as a doorway to conversation. Not interested, I shut him down quickly. I guess his pride was hurt because we wound up getting into a heated argument. I jumped chest to chest with him and began to point my fingers in his face, cussing like a sailor. My Brooklyn persona came blazing through. The entire cafeteria watched us. Finally, a friend of his named Paul came over and got between us. He talked me into calming down.

As I said before, I wasn't looking for a new dude. That was the last thing on my mind. But fresh out the gate, I liked Paul. He was cute and he was different from every other dude at Delaware State. He reminded me of the type of guys I dated back in New York: nice jewels, expensive clothes and smelled good too. He carried himself thuggishly. It was obvious he had something going on financially. I wasn't sure if the money was his or if it was coming from his family. Whatever the deal, it attracted me to him. My college plans of not having a boyfriend changed.

Of course there was an ulterior motive. Shit, Dame, Smiley and others— lots of others— had gotten me addicted to money. They got me addicted to living well. So of course, when I laid eyes on Paul, his pockets interested me just as much as he did. I'm not proud of it but it's just the way things were.

Paul and I began talking. He was feeling me just as much as I was him. He eventually invited me over to his spot

35

to cook for him, which I took him up on gladly. I wanted to see exactly what he had going on. He had a nice spot off campus filled with expensive furniture and a refrigerator full of food—every college student's dream. Anxious to get out of the dorm, I whipped my womanhood on him and practically moved myself into his place, purposely leaving my panties out in the open to mark my territory where the next bitch could see them, a technique I'd learned from Smiley. This all happened in two weeks. I know it sounds dumb. I didn't really even know this cat. But I was young back then so I was highly impatient and worked mainly on impulse. When I wanted what I wanted, I went for it, rarely thinking about consequences or anything else the future held. The wonder of being young, I guess.

I continued to keep my dorm room. I wasn't *that* naive. I wasn't going to be out in the cold if things possibly didn't work out between Paul and me. I was dumb…thankfully not that dumb. It wasn't long before Paul's secret was exposed. He was a drug dealer, a major one. He was hustling mainly back in Jersey every single weekend. Never broke, he had no problems spending on me. So the cash flow seemed plentiful since Dame was spending regularly on me too. I was loving it. And with Paul gone consistently every weekend that gave me time to cheat regularly with Dame. Everything was all good until my mother found out I'd moved in with Paul.

Man, my moms went straight bananas on me when she found out the news. I mean, she wouldn't let me hear the end of it. To this day, she still won't. She'd always beat into my head how important it was to go to college. She didn't want to see me on welfare and living in the projects knocked up at a young age with several kids like a lot of my friends were. She screamed on me about how most people who grew up in the projects ended up. She wanted more out of life for me and she wanted *me* to want the same.

In the end, my mom was so heated with me, she shut

me down. She stopped footing the bill for my education. She refused to pay for books, room and board or anything. She wouldn't even talk to me for weeks. It was a jolting reality check. One where you realize you're really on your own. Still I swore I knew everything there was to know about the world. I thought I had it all covered like most young, foolish women assume. Yet once you have to pay your own bills, you realize you didn't quite know everything you thought you did. The world gets a little colder, just like me.

For a moment, I had no idea exactly what I was going to do. I was in limbo. I panicked. Although I hadn't really been putting too much time and interest into college so far, knowing that I was in danger of losing it scared me. Quickly, I realized I had to get on my own grind. That was the New York part of me, that hustler mentality. I didn't want to rely on the money Dame was giving me, that was extra and couldn't be counted on. I got a job at Nations Bank.

Around this time, in 1998, things were growing even bigger for Dame and Roc-A-Fella. Jay's "Hard Knock Life" single was all over the radio and the video was all over BET and MTV. The album was flying off the store shelves. I even heard it blasting on campus a lot. To capitalize on the success, Dame announced the Hard Knock Life Tour, which would hit all the major colleges. My invite came quicker than expected. I said yes immediately, shrugging off my Friday and Monday classes often.

Rebel, as my mother would say.

The experience of kicking it on The Hard Knock Life Tour amazed me. I enjoyed riding on tour buses from city to city every night. I loved watching the Roc-A-Fella team performing on stage, perfecting their craft along with the newcomers trying to hold their own. It was like a dream to be a part of the growth and experience. It also gave me a chance to see that disrespectful side of Dame that people talked about often. We arrived at Morgan State with our usual entourage but the woman in charge said Nikeya and I couldn't come in with them. I watched Dame transform into the arrogant monster that everyone talks about. "If the girls don't come in, Jay doesn't perform." In hindsight I realize that was just a tactic. Clearly he wouldn't have stopped the show because of that. He could've just pulled out one of those crisp hundreds he often carried and ended the confrontation, but he liked showing his power. I started liking the power and fame too.

Back at Delaware State I became the focus. The new hype. After seeing me get dropped off on campus by a tour bus, they knew I knew Dame personally. Everyone had millions upon millions of questions. They wanted to know as much about Jay-Z, Memphis Bleek, and Amil as I could tell them. I loved the attention.

There were haters also. Some were jealous but for others, it was deeper than jealousy. It was real hatred in the truest definition of the word. Blacks, whites and even Latino students swore I was trying to act black. Some got buck, even attempting to clarify my racial status, like I wasn't clear on my heritage being one hundred percent Puerto Rican. I knew how to handle myself though. Shit, I'd been going through that since my toddler years.

For the record, I don't *act* black. I act like *myself.* I act like Winter. I just happened to have been raised around black people all my life. I was never raised around my own people so of course I'm going to act like what or who I've been always surrounded by. I've never gone out of my way to act that way. It just is what it is. It's just me being me.

Despite all the talk, Dame and I grew closer on the tour. Of course, since we were seeing each other on a regular basis, we were having sex more often, something I dreaded. But I was definitely feeling like we were going to take the relationship as far as it could go. Shit, I was being extra naive, even thinking eventually marriage. That's how close we were getting.

There was a downside to it all though. You can't turn down excitement. Spending so much time on the tour had me craving it constantly like crack or even good dick. Being away from it always made me feel like I was missing something. I couldn't concentrate on my studies. It had already been difficult enough dealing with college, knowing I truly didn't want to be there. The tour complicated that situation. I was missing Friday and Monday classes. I also wasn't studying and my enthusiasm for school work was diminishing.

Spending more time with Dame was beginning to show me a side of him I didn't like. More money and power had made him cocky and different from the Dame I'd come to know and crave to be around. He was screaming on a lot of people so I'd heard but luckily he never tried the bullshit on me. Still, he started missing my phone calls regularly. He was even getting a little too friendly with other chicks and didn't seem to care if it affected me. He'd say he wasn't fucking them but I didn't believe him. I had no proof though until one night while we were back at his penthouse lying in bed.

His bedroom door flew open. I just knew it was the police. The crashing sound from the door sent chills through me. Even for Dame, the macho image disappeared. His expression filled with fear not understanding how anyone could get into such a secured building. I assumed he thought it was the police too. Security wouldn't let anyone else upstairs.

"Nigga, I knew it!" some crazed woman I'd never seen before screamed at him from the edge of the bed. "I knew you were cheating, you lying muthafucka!"

Surprised, Dame jumped up and rushed her as she quickly began to make her way around the bed toward me. Strangely, I wasn't even afraid. For some reason I had the mentality that I belonged and she didn't. Even after realizing she was the mother of his first born who I thought was still

asleep in the room next to us, I didn't care. "You still fuckin'
them R&B chicks," she shouted! As she rambled on in a
rage, I quickly pulled the sheets tightly around my naked
body and jumped up also, ready to whip ass if need be. That
is until Dame and I both realized his son was awake and the
one who'd let her into the apartment.

Dame quickly grabbed her and took her from the room.
Somewhere in the apartment, I could still hear her for at least
several minutes going off on Dame until he finally got her
out of the house. That was the first sign that I wouldn't have
him to myself, ever. But the shit didn't stop there. The same
woman called a week later while I happened to be there. Although he went to another room to take the call, Dame put
the crazed woman on speakerphone. Once again she snapped
on him. This time she threatened to tell the whole Hip Hop
industry that he'd had liposuction, which I had no idea at the
time if it were even true. She also screamed about recently
catching him in bed with some R&B singer—that I'll leave
alone for now.

Dame's drama got to be too much for me. It was obvious he wasn't faithful to me and had no intentions of becoming so. Things became more open for me after that. That
experience made me grow up faster, recognizing my relationship with him for what it was. He used me and vice
versa. Unfortunately there was no controlling him. At times I
couldn't even reach him. It was cool, though, he was giving
me something better than his time: an education in GAME
101.

Trust no man.

5

Caught Up

Obviously, I wasn't a celebrity myself, far from it. But
among my friends and family I was beginning to feel like
one. Through mainly Dame, I was getting to attend more and
more industry events and my peoples knew it. They knew I'd
been spending less time at school. They were hitting me up
on a regular wanting to know when I was going to take them
with me to another party or wanting details about the ones I
couldn't take them to. It felt good to be the object of conversation. I enjoyed it. The night of Mase's album listening
party for Harlem World was no different.

The Roxy was packed. Everyone was there. Puffy was
sharpening his party throwing skills with each party he sponsored. He was upgrading with each. I guess it was because
he was gradually getting more and more money, making
more industry connections. Just like watching Dame grow, it
was interesting to see Puff do the same.

That night, as usual, I was enjoying myself. I was danc-
ing, talking to friends, getting my drink on and bobbing my
head to each of the songs the DJ was playing from Mase's
album. Sometime during that night, I noticed a guy looking
at me. He was surrounded by security so I knew he was

someone special or at least someone with some money. I did-
n't recognize him though. Going about my business, no matter where I was in the club or what I was doing, he kept
watching me. It was obvious that he was interested in me but
I didn't sweat it.

Dame and I were still together at that point. Obviously,
he had a lot of friends in the industry, some at the album release party. I didn't know who was possibly there keeping an
eye on me for Dame, if that was the case. But I did know that
Dame wasn't being faithful to me. I knew he was dating
other women so of course I felt it was only right that I be
able to do my thing also. If he could have a bitch on the side,
I could have a nigga. Fair exchange ain't no robbery.

Eventually, ole boy who'd been watching me all night
sent his security over to get me. They walked me over to
their boss and left us to talk. Looking back, it's weird realizing the moment he opened his mouth to me for the very first
time, the sound of his voice became an addiction I would
never be able to shake. It was raspy and had some sort of
strange effect on me that I can't explain to this day. It was
more than sexy.

Ole boy introduced himself as Jason. He was cute and
had a boyish look about him. His smile, even without fully
showing his teeth, was one of the brightest I've ever come
across. His head was shaved down to the scalp and smooth.
The entire package gave him a sort of innocence. I liked him
from the jump. After telling him my name, we began to talk.
"Winter," he laughed. I'd always thought my name was a
curse. It's the type of name that makes people interested in
you. He seemed interested in discovering more about me
than discussing himself. He wanted to know who I was with,
what college I was attending, where I was from. It all
seemed to intrigue him. I liked that so we eventually exchanged numbers.

Jason and I talked on the phone nearly every day despite the fact that I still lived with Paul. I enjoyed his conversation and he seemed to enjoy mine. It got to the point that I was looking forward to his calls, breaking my neck to answer whenever I knew he was calling. Hearing his raspy voice was like a fix. One day, Jason told me he was packing up and hitting the road. Not sure what he meant, I asked where he was going and why.

"You know the song, 'We'll Always Love Big Poppa'?" he asked.

Of course I knew it. Who in New York didn't?

"Yeah, I know the song," I told him.

"That's me and my group, The Lox. I'm a rapper. I'm Jadakiss."

I was totally caught off guard. In all honesty, at that moment in my life, getting with rappers wasn't by design. It wasn't something I planned. It was all coincidence or maybe even fate. I hadn't got with Nino because he was a rapper and obviously I had no idea Dame was a Hip Hop CEO when I met him. The shit had all fallen into my lap, like it was all God's design. It was as if the Hip Hop world was coming after me, not the other way around.

After that phone conversation, Jason hit the road and stayed on it a lot but he never stopped calling me. If anything, he started calling *more*, excitedly telling me about everything he was experiencing. He was seeing the world for the very first time and it had him eager for more. He was like a kid in a candy store or a child on Christmas morning. I was genuinely happy for him. We became very good friends.

Jason wasn't from the projects like me. He was from a safe part of Yonkers so he wasn't as gutter as me or most dudes I'd associated with. He had even gone to college himself. That was cool though. If anything, it made me like him more. We didn't go on traditional dates. It was more like we'd simply meet up at events, usually with my girl Nikeya tagging along, and have fun. We rarely had privacy because he and I always had our crews with us, wanting them to share in the fun we were having in the industry. That's what it was all about at that time….Fun. We were young.

I didn't love Jason but I definitely had strong feelings for him, feelings that could've possibly turned into love. Being around him was something I always looked forward to. Even our sex was more playful than anything else back then. We couldn't really get it in exactly how we wanted to because our peoples were always around so we had to sneak it in closets and back seats. We even had to lock Nikeya's ass out of a hotel room once so we could at least get a quickie in.

Then there were the times where we really got it in, with Jason showing off his mandingo skills. He was good in bed, the cuddly type. He knew how to be affectionate yet handled his business leaving me satisfied. Just the fact that he thought enough of me to offer a rag afterwards or asked me if I was hungry, thirsty, or needed anything should've told me to try to keep things working with him. It was rare to see a rapper with emotions like that. He even made me want to do better in the emotion department. I'll say this, if he ever goes broke, he could bottle his sex up and sell it for a sizable amount of money. Yeah…it was that good.

We'd even sneak and freak out in one of the bunks on the tour bus while everyone else was sleep or hanging out in the living room near the front part of the bus. Those were the good days with him. He was *Jason* to me, not *Jadakiss*. He was genuine and appreciative of his opportunity. Money wasn't flowing back then but he didn't seem to care. He was just happy to have his shot and he wanted me to be a part of it. He wanted me to experience his climb to fame alongside him. On one of the weekends Paul was away, Jason performed at Delaware State. The shit made me an instant celebrity. Everybody knew because of the way I dressed and because of my swagger, something about me wasn't quite like them. When they saw me receiving special treatment from Jadakiss, which I was careful to make look like a friendship so Paul wouldn't ask questions, my stock went up even further than before. Everybody rode me hard, wanting to be in my circle. I loved the attention Jason brought me, but loved his personality more. He was very humorous and fun. I was really thinking about cutting Dame loose and being with Jason.

I had no agenda or ulterior motives for spending time with Jason. Although money always came in from dudes I dated, I really wanted Jason's friendship. That was good enough for me even though he sent me money through Western Union often. At one point my second semester of college tuition was due plus books, and all my other expenses, both personal and traveling expenses. As usual Jason came through just like the others.

I guess me and Jason were just kids then who were just genuinely happy to be a part of something so huge. That was why we clicked. We both wanted happiness and fun out of life. It seemed like we were meant to be.

There was guilt, though. Keeping it one hundred with myself, I have to admit that Dame was still in the picture. He shouldn't have been. He didn't deserve to be. It was obvious that for him I was just one girl in a thousand, whereas with Jason I was his *only.* When I look back, I feel horrible about that. I should've let Dame go but I didn't know how to.

Jason and his group began to blow up. Lil Kim and DMX appeared on their "Money, Power & Respect" track. That song was like crack. Everyone loved it and The Lox's rhyme skills were being praised. Everyone in the industry was calling them real Hip Hop. The shit was even swelling my head up. There was nothing like being around my friends when his records would come on Hot 97. It felt good to hear people acknowledging that same distinctive raspy voice that had turned me on from the very first moment I'd heard it.

This was Bad Boy's heyday so Jason being signed with

them was perfect. Everything the label touched was going platinum. Jason was being poised to do the same and he knew it. I was just as happy for his success. So when he invited me to meet him in Philly on the Bad Boy "No Way Out" tour, I accepted quickly. Nikeya and I left school and hopped the first thing smoking to Philly. When we got there, we met him at his hotel where there were about twenty other rappers and staff members ready to hop in the motorcade. Within minutes of walking into his room, it was time to roll. Soon we were hopping into a tinted out van and headed to the venue with Puff leading us in a Bentley. In front of him was a major police escort.

Man, it was like some Obama shit!

Jason had come up. Immediately, I noticed how Jason was being treated on this tour. He was becoming more of a priority. Since The Lox were now obviously becoming the next best thing, they were being treated that way.

When we reached the venue, I couldn't believe my eyes. I mean, what I'd experienced with Dame and the college tour shows was wild. But this right here was fuckin' mind blowing! The arena was huge. Brand new tour buses. Expensive equipment. Cameras. A heart shaped bed was unloaded, strictly for Lil Kim. Everyone had an assistant. Even the assistants had assistants. Security was all over the place. Dozens of Philadelphia police officers were also there. The moment seemed larger than life. It was like watching a movie being made.

After Jason left us so he could go get prepared, Nikeya and I slipped on our backstage passes and headed directly backstage. Seeing what was going on behind the curtains was even more mind blowing than what we'd seen outside. Everyone was back there: Black Rob, Nas, Busta Ryhmes, Mase, and a whole lot of others. Somewhere between my seventeenth and nineteenth birthday I'd screwed Mase so seeing him felt uncomfortable. It was unmemorable so pretending as if he never drooled on my back during sex was best for us both. We both just waved and kept it moving.

I saw Kim also. Seeing her felt weird. I could remember her days at the Junior Mafia house. She was just a regular girl back then. Now she was all over the radio and everyone was making a huge fuss over her. I wanted to approach her and ask her if she remembered me from the house but decided not to. I was happy for her though. She'd dealt with Big's death and turned it into a come up, repping him every time she got the chance and doing everything she could to keep his legacy and memory alive. Nikeya and I were having fun though. We couldn't stop smiling and laughing. Nothing could fuck it up, at least that was what I'd thought just before my eyes landed on a familiar but unexpected face.

Dame was there.

We were in a crowded hallway when I noticed him. Immediately, my heart rose to my throat. I didn't know what the hell to do. I didn't know if I should run, duck or hide. I should've known this was going to happen eventually. Sooner or later. I guess being so young and new to the game, it hadn't occurred to me how small the industry was.

Come to find out, Jay-Z was performing on the tour also. Since Nikeya and I came at the spur of the moment, we had no idea. Man, my heart was pounding at that moment. Within just seconds of me seeing him, Dame spotted me. I swallowed hard when a surprised look spread across his face. Without hesitation, he made his way through the crowded hallway with a vicious strut directly towards me, never taking his eyes off me.

"What are you doing here?" he asked as soon as he reached me.

In that brief moment, Jason's face crossed my mind. I saw his smile in my head. In my ears, I heard his voice. I saw all the good times we had and were having. I didn't want to lose that. I wanted that forever. But at the same time, the selfish side of me didn't want to lose what I had with Dame, although it wasn't much. I wanted to have my cake and eat it too so I did exactly what Dame had taught me...

I lied.

"One of The Lox is Nikeya's cousin," I said with my face twisted into a smirk.

Dame didn't respond. He just gave me this kind of sideways sort of look, obviously knowing I was lying. He'd been in the industry long enough to recognize "game." But instead of speaking on it, he simply looked me up and down, turned around and walked off. I had no idea if he believed me or not. Something told me he didn't. I wasn't sure but the chance of wedding bells ringing seemed to dwindle.

6   **Bamboozled**

Have you ever been somewhere where people are telling you that you're supposed to be but inside your heart, you know you're not supposed to be there? Well, that's how I felt about college. I know it was supposed to be about getting an education and all that good shit. But college isn't for everyone, myself included. At least, that's how I felt by the end of my sophomore year. God, I hated that place every second I was there.

I felt like I was inside a shell. I didn't have anything in common with most of my fellow students. Although most of us came from the hood, we hadn't come from the same place. We couldn't really relate to each other. When I look back now, it was obvious that I was just young, immature and missing the spotlight I'd grown used to, especially when I would watch Hip Hop videos, award shows, and interviews. My longtime friend Ayanna from Brooklyn was dating Spliff Star so listening to her tell me places Spliff and Busta traveled to excited me. The shit always had me feeling like I was missing out on something, not realizing I was blessed for being able to get an education. I was worrying about the wrong things.

Mingling with college kids was no match for kicking it with celebrities. College life couldn't compare with life on a tour bus. I was used to seeing new cities and meeting new important people. I was used to parties and rubbing elbows with the entertainment elite. I was used to everything and everyone around me moving fast. On the Hard Knock Life Tour I was a part of Hip Hop history as it was being written. In college, I was confined to a damn campus like I was in prison or something. It was too silent and slow. The difference between my current life and the life I wanted to go back to was too extreme.

My major in Nursing took boring to another level, it was nothing like I'd expected or hoped. The classes were like watching paint dry. The job at the bank was so super lame I wanted to get up and walk out. I only stayed because I knew I really had no other choice if I was going to be independent. Mom still wasn't checking for me financially because of the Paul situation. I knew if I begged her and gave her the puppy dog eyes, she'd come through like any mother would for their child but I was determined to stand on my own. I had gotten so used to being on my own that I had developed pride. I couldn't go back to her and ask for money without feeling like less than a woman. Besides, Paul was taking care of the bills and Jason covered everything else. Of course I still had Dame in one of those bottles where you cracked it open upon an emergency. Most people know how it goes: you use to get used. Even though I had all of that going on, I knew how important it was to stay in school. My Aunt Leslie had become my role model, graduating with a degree in Nursing. She was the reason why I'd chosen Nursing as a major in the first place. Still, I felt unsatisfied.

Although I liked Paul and lived with him, I was more interested in his money. Yeah, the shit sounds foul but it is what it is. With Jason, I had strong feelings, something I hadn't experienced since Smiley. The last thing I wanted him to think was that I wanted him for his celebrity status or his money. Don't get me wrong. Those things were nice too but I wanted his heart much more. Jason and I had clearly clicked. We were friends *first*...the lovers thing was secondary. There was no feeling in the world like that. I definitely didn't want to lose it.

Dame was in the shadows also. I was still fucking with him. But the situation was similar to the one I had with Paul, just a little more complicated. Obviously, since Dame had much more money and he was becoming a force to be reckoned with in the music industry, I tried to keep things tighter with him than Paul. But all that changed in the spring of 1999.

I was driving through Harlem one day, happy to be in New York. I'd been back from college for a little over a week. As I was driving, I saw Dame's Bentley double parked in front of a barber shop. That was one of the things that always turned me on about Dame. Although he was making moves in the music industry and appearing in videos, he still kept it hood. Most rappers and executives sign that contract, move to the suburbs and never look back. Some act like they're scared of where they come from. Dame wasn't like that. He didn't fear being in the streets that had created him. If anything, he felt right at home there.

Anyway, I hurried to find a parking spot, anxious to meet up. Every time I got with him, a shopping spree, a meal at an expensive restaurant or something out of the ordinary was almost always a given. I couldn't wait to get with him this time. Besides, my bags that I'd left with him earlier in the week were still in the trunk of his car. I pulled to the curb and parked right behind him. He was coming out of the shop as I was turning off my car. As usual, his gear was crisp and his jewels were shining. It was always that way with him. You would *never* catch Dame looking any other way.

I hopped out of my car. He saw me and immediately headed towards me as I made my way around the hood of my car to the curb happy to see him. He instantly began ushering me back towards the rear of my car in a hurry. When we reached it I looked in his face and could see something strange in his eyes, something I'd never seen in them before.

"My girl's in the car," he said before I could say a word.

Disbelief spread through my veins. I felt hot inside. I looked at his car….then back at him….then towards the car again. From where we were standing, I could see the back of some female's head over the headrest of the passenger seat. I wanted to spaz the fuck out. Yeah, I was fucking him, Jason and Paul. Yeah, it was all possibly karma coming to bite my ass. And? So what?

At that point my flaws didn't matter. He'd gotten caught.

My eyes saw red.

"Your girl!" I yelled at him.

"Yeah, my girl," he returned nonchalantly.

The way he said it made me stare at him for a moment. He placed gangsta type emphasis on '*My Girl*,' like he was married to the chick or something, like he hadn't just been banging my head into the headboard recently. He'd turned into Dr. Jekyll/Mr. Hyde again.

For a moment, I couldn't react. I couldn't speak. I was pissed off. Adrenaline pumped through my veins. I wanted to haul off and knock Dame to the ground especially when I realized I was just in that front seat four days ago. That same arrogant expression on his face told me it was just the way it was, and I had to accept it. Surprisingly, the girl in the front seat never got out. I never saw her face, and it never dawned on me to step to her. I guess because Dame had just confirmed my status. Finally, despite my pain and pride, I said, "Dame, I just want my clothes out of your car."

Dame popped the trunk, gave me my clothes and I left. As I pulled away from the curb a part of me wanted to shout out in rage or kick some shit around. I felt like a damn idiot, like I needed to cry to show I'd been punked, but not a single tear would fall. Once again, my heart hardened. This was the first time another woman had been put in front of me.

Needless to say, I fell all the way back from Dame's ass after that. We still talked but things were different...way different. Months passed and he became less available. Even Paul too. Whatever exactly Paul had going on regarding his grind, it must've been good because he was still spending every weekend away from Delaware and never attempted to spend one weekend with me. He was probably cheating too. He'd never gotten caught but I didn't trust him. I trusted no one.

My mother's words rang in my head: "Men will be men, Winter."

Jason, on the other hand, I treasured. He was becoming my heart. Since Paul was gone more often, that gave me time to get with Jason a lot more. As far as I had seen, Jason wasn't fucking with other chicks. He hadn't quite got to the level where groupies were all over him yet. And he was still down to earth, still cool. Even without Dame's big pockets, I preferred him over Dame.

Guilt filled my heart when I was with him. I felt like I was playing him when he didn't deserve to be played. He'd never crossed me. He'd always been real but I wasn't being real with him. Although we weren't quite an official item— our relationship bordered between friendship with the possibility of something more—he still deserved to know what he was getting into. I didn't want to hurt him. I couldn't tell him though. I just couldn't.

I wanted to have my cake and eat it too, I guess. That's always been my damn problem. I wanted to keep all three men in my life for selfish reasons, even if it meant hurting the one I really had strong feelings for. But a few months later of that same year, I was forced to finally cut one of those men loose.

One night, I was watching an awards show. Jay-Z received an award. I was proud of him. He was doing his thing that year. Then he said something that made my heart plunge to my stomach…

Jay congratulated Dame on the birth of his new baby girl.

My stomach dropped to the floor like I was on a rollercoaster ride. In a sense…I was. Of course, I knew there had been other bitches. I knew Dame wasn't being faithful. But a *baby*? Are you serious? I was in absolute shock behind that shit. Especially after my phone started ringing and someone told me the female's name was Rachel Roy. All women want their men to cheat with someone wack so we can talk shit. I couldn't. And I even thought about the fact that she was probably the chick in the car that day.

Obviously, I shouldn't have been pissed. I shouldn't have given it space to rent inside my head. I was playing him and he'd been playing me. Still, though, it just didn't seem fair. I felt like I had been played worse. I felt like he had gotten the best of me. After taking all his wet saliva all that time.

When I spoke to Dame a few weeks later, I wanted to see him face-to-face so I could slap the shit out of him. But we just talked via phone. I simply said, "What, nigga, you couldn't tell me? I've been messing with you for over a year. Didn't I deserve to know you was having a baby?"

As if my feelings meant nothing, he said without remorse, "That could've been you, Winter, but you wanted to go to college."

Stunned by his answer, those words were all I needed. Those words were my wake-up call. From that point, my motto basically became, "Get what you can get from these niggas, Winter, before they hurt you first." I couldn't love another man. I couldn't take a chance on getting played again. I can't say that I didn't learn a lot from Dame during my time with him. A lot of what I learned follows me in business today but he also taught me to be leery of men. They may wine and dine you but that doesn't mean you're special. You could be one in a million.

Still, despite the heartaches, I kept hanging onto the thought that just maybe someone in that world would marry me. Even though I had seen the worst, there were always signs that I could have a healthy relationship with somebody I would be able to really love and have fame and fortune with. Like my long-time friend Ayanna. When I got word that she was pregnant by the man of her dreams, the news made me think hard about relationships once again.

Ayanna had gotten pregnant, out of wedlock by Spliff Star, who was Busta Rhymes hype man and closest homie. I immediately had worries. I'd known Spliff for years. The two of us were crazy tight and had a bond between us that I cherished. In fact, it was that bond that made me warm up more to males than females. The two of us were just that cool with each other, him always looking out for my best interest and telling me how guys really think. I guess that was why I was so tight with so many dudes. Because of Spliff, I gave them all the benefit of the doubt.

But I still had reservations about Ayanna's pregnancy. It was happening at the wrong time. Ayanna wasn't ready for a child. Shit, she was in the exact same position I was in: no money, going to college, immature and partying every night. That wasn't going to work. But most importantly, she had a misconception of what being the wife and baby mama of a rapper was all about. All she saw were the clothes, money, spotlight and parties. She didn't know what happened behind the curtains and underneath the tables. Most rappers didn't have the money people thought they had. Also, since they're entertainers, they're never home and rarely faithful. Ayanna would basically be stuck with a child she'd most likely have to raise on her own the best way she could. Spliff was my dude and I hated to imagine he might be that way, but I'd been around enough cats in the industry to know what was what.

Ayanna's reality was going to change drastically. She'd probably have to drop out of school. And as in love with Spliff as she was, she would probably depend on him for support. I knew the worst was yet to come. As time went by, she began to see for herself. While she was stuck in her dorm room, she began to hear about Spliff's partying and womanizing. She got a chance to see for herself what it was like to call her man's phone and not get an answer. She was getting a dose of what it really was like to be the girlfriend of a rapper. She also thought Spliff wasn't financially well off. Fact is, he was. He just didn't share his money with her. It hurt me to know Spliff hadn't kept it one hundred with Ayanna but there was nothing I could do. Their relationship was their relationship. I loved them both and didn't want to come in between them.

All in all though, Spliff really did love Ayanna. I could hear it in his voice and see it in his eyes. He really was crazy about her. And despite everything she was learning about him, Ayanna felt the same way. Their love was deep. It reminded me of what I had with Smiley. And since I loved both of them, I supported them and helped plan the wedding after Spliff proposed.

Eventually, both the baby and the wedding came. Both moments were special and memorable to me. I became a proud godmother the day their son entered the world and Spliff chose Busta to be his best man at the wedding. The groomsmen looked their part, extra fly dressed in cream suits and Timbos. Jaws dropped when everyone saw them.

That time in my life was a peaceful one. Both of my

best friends were in love with each other and it seemed to be working out. I was also good with Busta and The Flipmode Squad. We were all family, although many people thought me and Busta were fucking. We all spent a few Christmas' and Thanksgivings together but that was it. Nothing sexual ever happened. It never even crossed my mind, real talk.

From a distance, I watched Ayanna and Spliff's marriage. I admired their love for each other. Despite the problems of the industry, they were fighting hard to make it work. Damn, I wanted that or something similar. I wanted someone I could come home to. I wanted that badly but I just wasn't ready for the tradeoff. Too much had to be invested. A committed relationship meant leaving myself open for the pain. Besides, my love for Hip Hop had gotten deeper. There was no turning back.

7   Game Changer

A few years passed by. I like to think that I matured over those years. The Dame episode forced me to. At twenty years old, I'd changed. I wasn't the only one though. Jason and everything between us had begun to change also. We weren't kids anymore.

Jason had begun to transform into a Hip Hop celebrity. He had become Jadakiss to everyone around him. He was now too famous to be Jason to me anymore. Because of that, things between us were no longer the same. The invites to meet him on the road stopped. The sharing rooms with six to eight people stopped. The laughing, joking, partying and being happy to be a part of something that seemed bigger than us had stopped. There was no more fun. His life was now filled with shows, interviews, security, photo sessions and a whole lot more. We still kept in touch but we were growing apart, taking different directions in life. It hurt me because I had always wanted things between us to stay the way they were before the fame, but life is full of change and it was about to bring even more into my life in the form of someone from my past I hadn't seen coming.

Several years back, there was this skinny kid from my

hood that I never really paid any attention. We had seen each other around but never really talked. Back then, I was dating this dude from the Brevoort projects in Brooklyn named Quan. Both he and Quan ran in the same circles even though this kid was younger than him. That was to the extent to how he knew me—nothing more, nothing less. I'd never been interested enough to even ask his name. It wasn't that he wasn't cute or anything. He was. We just never felt the need to know each other's name. That's why even to this day, it's still hard to believe that little skinny dude would eventually become famous and the two of us would become very good friends.

Anyway, this same skinny kid pulled up on me at a club one evening several years later. He introduced himself to me as Fab. At that time, he was in the beginning stages of his successful career. The first thing I noticed about him was his smile, chipped tooth and full lips. They were hot I admitted to myself silently. He worked them attractively as he talked to me. My eyes couldn't leave them. We soon exchanged numbers.

That night, I was under the impression that Fab wanted to get at me. The way he spoke, his body language, his words; all of it was smooth and attractive. Besides, how often does a man exchange numbers with a female without intending to get much more? After two weeks of talking on the phone and exchanging two way pages, he never said in exact words that he wanted to hook up with me. The conversation seemed more like the type two friends would have with each other. Still, I felt he had a crush on me.

At the time, Fab was on a promo run for his new single "Can't Deny It." He was traveling from city to city. When he was headed back to New York, he hit me up and wanted to hook up. By then I'd gotten a 2000 silver Honda Accord coupe funded from my dudes, but mostly from Paul. I drove from Delaware back to NYC to pick up him and his man-

agers, Cheo and Webb, from Newark Airport. I knew Cheo
and Webb from my younger days so I felt comfortable
around them, especially Webb. We'd had a lot of dealings
with one another, where we all chilled together, so it seemed
only right. Also, Fab and I weren't sleeping together so we
were just homies kickin' it like we'd done back in the hood.
From the airport we drove through Queens to their two
bedroom apartment. Now, obviously, after everything I'd
seen and every one I'd been around in the industry, I had
high expectations for Fab's apartment. I was expecting floor
to ceiling windows, sunken marble floors, expensive wall to
wall furniture, walk-in closets full of clothes, two-storied
ceilings. I expected his shit to be hot. After all, he had a song
and video getting major airplay all over the radio and television.

Boy, was I wrong.

The spot resembled little more than a hole in the wall.
There was absolutely *no* living room furniture. Clothes, dirty
socks and sneakers were thrown everywhere. The kitchen
sink was filled with dirty dishes. Flies were all over the
place. Fab's bedroom consisted of a mattress sitting on the
floor and a box fan in the window. There was absolutely
nothing *Fabulous* about Fab's spot. The place was disgust-
ing.

I don't know why I did it. Maybe it was just the woman
in me, but I put on some rubber gloves and started cleaning
the house without anyone asking me to do so. The guys
looked at me like I was crazy. I didn't care. I just felt like
maybe my cleanliness would rub off on them. By the time I
was done, the entire spot smelled like Pine Sol.

Even though the accommodations weren't the best,
since it didn't bother the guys, it didn't bother me. Since I
cleaned it, I was able to deal with it. Besides, if I could get
used to a dorm full of funky broads, I could deal with an
apartment that housed three dudes. Shit, if anything, I en-

joyed myself. Everything was sweet. We sat on the hard
floors eating Chinese food, talking Hip Hop, watching
movies and just vibing until we fell asleep. That night, I slept
on the mattress with Fab. Think what you want but that's *all*
we did on that mattress. Sleep.

The next morning came around. Fab had some things
he needed to do in the city. His record label, Elektra, had
booked him at a nice hotel. I drove him and the others to the
hotel and waited. After they checked in, we all rolled out
again and headed to the studio. Just like the night before at
the apartment, I just fell in place. They treated me like I was
one of them. They never tried anything. When they passed
the blunt, I was included in the rotation. When they poured a
cup, they made sure mine was filled too. They didn't bite
their tongues about anything so I didn't bite mine neither.
After all, we were all basically from the same hood so I had
no problem being me. That meant letting my hair down and
cussing just like them. That was the way it went from then
on.

Of course, people we ran into talked and whispered. I
wasn't on payroll and I wasn't any of their girlfriends so
people wondered if I was a groupie. They wondered if I was
fucking all three of them, especially Fab. But, shit, people
talked about Jesus. It didn't bother me. The three treated me
like their sister. What other people thought was their own
business. Although, in my mind, I had to sometimes wonder
what exactly I was doing there.

Fab, on the other hand, treated me a little more differently than his managers did. He was playful and always
smiling at me but never took it further than that. I was just as
playful with him, always looking for a reason to nudge him
or be near him. I could always tell there was something more
behind his smile. It was obvious but I just assumed he was
shy and would tell me what was up when he was ready. It
was cute to me.

One morning he did something I didn't quite know how to take. He woke up, got ready and kissed me on my forehead. He was gone before I could ask him why he'd done it. I just sat there wondering. It made me smile. It was obvious he liked me but for whatever his reasons were, he just didn't want to say it. I noticed in public, he was always free but when it was just me and him, he would get nervous. I don't know what it was. Maybe I intimidated him somehow. I'm not sure. I now know that those three days we spent together and moments like that one would eventually change.

Later that day, we met up at his photo shoot. From there, we hopped into my ride and headed to a press conference. Throughout that day, Fab gave several interviews and free-styled every time someone asked him to, eager to show off his skills. It was at that moment that I became a fan. I liked "Can't Deny It" like everyone else but hearing him freestyle took the shit to another level. I was amazed. He could spit about anything anyone would ask him at the drop of a dime. And it all sounded as hot as if he had written it the day before.

Just like Jason, he was happy to finally be given the chance to let the whole world know how talented he was. The past three days of living in an average apartment didn't bother him. Eating lunch, breakfast and dinner on the floor didn't bother him. Being broke didn't bother him. There was no ego. He had that innocence that most artists have when they're coming into the game just before success sinks its claws into them and turns them into egotistical ass monsters that you can't stand to be around.

After an interview, DJ Clue, who I already knew at the time, stopped by and told Fab he had a surprise for him.

"What is it?" Fab asked with that smile I liked.

"We have to go to Queens to get it."

Fab and his manager rolled out and told me they would be right back. A couple hours later, they returned in a brand new black Mercedes Coupe. My mouth dropped. That moment changed something in me. Seeing Fab happy made me happy. But that was one of those key moments in my life where I can put a finger on it and say, "Something changed."

A moment ago, Fab didn't have a penny to his name, just a closet full of jerseys. He was living in a hole in the wall. He didn't have anything but his talent to rhyme. Three days later, he was whipping a brand new Benz because of that talent. It was at that moment that I was no longer satisfied with just wanting to be a part of Hip Hop. I wanted more. I wanted to be a mover and shaker in the game. I wanted to make decisions and sign checks. I decided to listen and pay attention to the mechanics and the ins and outs of the game. I understood that was where the real money was.

The next morning, we got dressed. Fab hopped in his Benz, I hopped in my Accord and we made plans to get with each other later. It didn't happen though. Needless to say, Fab blew up. His success kept him busy and his name grew. We would see each other at events and parties. Sometimes we would speak, other times we didn't. He would always text me right after those moments and ask me why I didn't speak. That shit was childish to me. I never understood it. Success was changing him like it changed everybody. Sometimes I'd respond to his texts, other times I wouldn't. He still had a special place in my heart though. Every time I'd see him in his videos showing off his money and cars, I couldn't help but smile, remembering those three days in that raggedy apartment when he had nothing. I'll always treasure those times.

I went on with my life, realizing my time would come eventually. Finally, it did. My home girl, Janine, who I'd known for years, had to drop off some paperwork one day to Anton Marchand, who was rapper Foxy Brown's brother and manager. While I was waiting for Janine in the lounge of the studio where the photo shoot was taking place, I met a girl named Kiersten, an independent stylist. We small talked for a moment and she told me about her job. She talked about the cities and countries she'd been to and the people she'd worked with detailing all of the glamour. I listened intently to every word. I knew then that styling was what I wanted to do.

Kiersten and I swapped information and kept in touch. She eventually allowed me to assist her on styling jobs on the weekends. I would drive up from Delaware to New York and bask in my new passion. We worked with high end clients from outside the Hip Hop world, people I didn't know anything about like Laura Linney and Javier Bardem. We styled them for the cover of *L.A Magazine*. We also worked on issues for *The Source, XXL, Italian Vogue* and even shopped for Britney Spears. The experience meant a lot to me and I learned so much from Kiersten about the basics of styling.

Styling Laura Linney in Alice & Olivia and Fred Leighton jewelry impressed me the most. That jewelry is considered estate jewelry causing us to have insurance just to walk into the store to pull pieces. It was my first experience seeing that designers allow you to come into their showroom and borrow thousand dollar pieces. Jimmy Choo sending Kiersten 20 to 30 pair of shoes all thrown in a shopping bag sent by messenger excited me too. Along with the fact that when we worked big jobs we would have a car service driving us around the city as we did our pulls.

Despite all the newness and excitement, I remained in school. I felt the fashion vibe so much that I changed my major the next semester from Nursing to Fashion Merchandising, eager to suck up as much about the craft as possible. Fashion became my new drug. And I knew becoming a stylist was what I was destined to do.

Finally, I had discovered exactly what I wanted out of life. I had discovered a way to create my own identity and make my own way. I would finally be able to break into not only the Hip Hop world that I loved so much, but also the entertainment world period. It was finally going to happen. I was happy and couldn't wait to find out where my career decision was going to lead. But little did I know, I wasn't going to like where it would take me.

8   Power Move

Like that old song, "Love Don't Live Here Anymore," relationships weren't a priority for me anymore. And catching feelings for any man was *definitely* out of the question. I had been played and made a fool of by too many of them. Relationships proved to be a waste of time and energy in my book. I just didn't have time for the disappointment it brought. If anything, I'd grown extra heartless.

It may be wrong to say but after all I'd been through with the male species, especially in the industry, all they could do for me at that point was pay my bills and occasionally eat me. I was out for self. If I decided to fuck with a man, he would serve a purpose. There would be no love on the horizon. It would be about money and that's it. Shit, why not? I had to invest in my future, not a man.

Besides myself, all I had love for was styling at that point. It was the first thing in my life that I'd come across and wanted to do every day. It didn't seem like work because I enjoyed it so much. I threw myself into it, thinking about it night and day. I ate, slept and shitted the craft just like Dame had done Roc-A-Fella. I hated college so majoring in styling was the only thing there that made attending worth my while. I wanted to be the best at it.

School taught me a lot about styling but I was learning much more from my mentor, Kiersten. She was actually giving me on the job training and experience, and I was coming along fast. We became good friends so I felt comfortable talking to her about pulling outfits for Foxy Brown. Although Foxy wasn't a top priority for her, she agreed. Styling Foxy was cool because she wanted the best high end designers like Chanel, Gucci, Prada, La Perla, and Christian Louboutins—this was long before they became popular in the hood.

In 2002 on one of my weekends back in New York, we styled Foxy for The VMAs. We pulled Dior and Gucci gowns and H Stern jewelry for her for the MTV awards. I had become so passionate about the designers Kiersten worked with.

The situation was super exciting for me. Just being around the hype was like a drug. I loved the feeling. I knew for a fact that this was my calling. I wanted to feel like this for the rest of my life. The only thing I didn't like was the diva attitudes I came across occasionally.

I quickly learned Foxy wasn't sitting at the bottom of Kiersten's priority list simply because her name wasn't as big as most of her other clients. She was there because of her attitude and how unprofessional she acted. She often showed her ass. I experienced it that night.

For whatever reason, Foxy was running late. She hadn't done a fitting. She just assumed she could fit the sample sizes, which was a mistake. She arrived at the hotel just an hour before she needed to be on the red carpet, which was a complete no-no. We had to work hard and fast to get her ready. Shit, it took two hours of trying on clothes just to find something she could fit. The entire time, she complained like it was our fault there was such a problem, when in reality, if she'd done the fittings earlier like she was supposed to, everything would have been all good. While getting her ready, her brother Gavin called. She immediately put him on speaker phone. He asked her who was with her. When she mentioned my name, he recognized me and said, "What up, Winter?"

I had known Gavin from hanging with Fab and my Brevoort crew. He told Foxy he knew me. After that, her attitude changed. Well, it changed towards *me* at least. When she hung up, she asked me how I knew her brother. I told her and we began to talk. Through the conversation, I discovered she and I had once gone to the same night school in Brooklyn. It always seemed crazy to others that I would attend classes at night even though my grades were on point. But for me it made perfect sense. It's where all the guys with money hung out, the ones I remained attracted to. I made sure to be there and Foxy did too so we knew a lot of the same people. We began to click. But, it wasn't quite the same for Kiersten.

I don't know why or what Foxy's beef with her was all about. Foxy yelled and ranted at her, calling her out of her name…she even used the word 'bitch.' She treated Kiersten like pure *shit*. She was never nice to her at all. She talked down to her and would make her cry at times. Kiersten told me Foxy even threatened to send her brother to her house to beat her up. Kiersten was super terrified. I had to reassure her that I knew her brother and that she didn't have to worry.

When I look at how Foxy's promising career fizzled so quickly, it was obvious why. Kiersten wasn't the only person Foxy treated like that. A lot of people caught Foxy's attitude, some she even physically assaulted. She developed a reputation for it. Maybe she felt her success gave her the right to dog people and disrespect them whenever she felt like it. I think that attitude played a huge part in her downfall. You can't treat people like that and stay successful no matter how talented you are.

Eventually, Kiersten dropped Foxy as a client. Although Foxy and I were cool because of Gavin, my loyalty was with Kiersten. She was my mentor. She got me into this game. When Kiersten left, I went with her. It turned out to be a good decision. Through my time with her, I soon found myself getting deeper and deeper in the styling world. I was learning more, meeting important people and stock piling contacts that could help take my career to a new level. One of those people was DanTan, Head of Marketing for Murder Inc.

I ran into DanTan around Christmas of 2002. I was with Janine who mentioned to him that I'd started styling. He let me know he was currently looking for someone to style Irv Gotti, Ja Rule and Ashanti. One thing led to another and I got the job.

Excited isn't a strong enough description of how I felt. There isn't a word in the English dictionary that can describe it. I found myself hanging around the Murder Inc. crew and getting to know everyone. They loved my sassy, quick at the tongue personality, and the feeling was mutual. They soon became like family.

My new job demanded a lot of my time so I quit my banking job in Delaware. I was still enrolled in college but only part-time. Although my interest wasn't there, I wouldn't allow myself to drop out. Maybe, deep inside, I knew I wouldn't be able to face my mother if I did.

By February, I was ready to style on my own. The first Murder Inc. artists I styled were Ja Rule and Ashanti for Total Request Live (TRL), a show on MTV. It was a Valentine's Day special one that remains a distinct memory for me today. I was nervous without Kiersten being my first time officially on my own. Although I knew I was ready and had strong confidence in my skills, there was still that part of me that questioned my ability. There was that part of me that said I might fuck up the opportunity. The pressure was on and I could feel it. But I knew I had to suck it up and do my thing.

I didn't know if I was walking into a mess….or if they'd shoot me crazy looks. Sometimes artist didn't like the clothes a new stylist would bring them, and I had no clue if my choices would even fit them right. They barely knew me and certainly didn't know if they could trust my skills. Thankfully, I came through with flying colors.

Working on Ja Rule was a completely different experience from working with Foxy. Ja was super *huge* at the time. His songs and videos were all over the radio and television but it didn't seem to be a big deal with him. He was down to earth and treated everyone with respect. He was the type who always checked on others, making sure everyone was okay, never allowing the money or fame to go to his head. And with me, he treated me like a part of the family; one of the fellas.

My career was taking off. Sometimes I'd make up to fifteen hundred dollars a day. My work was extending even past Murder Inc. with small independent jobs, but Irv and his label were where my heart was. They embraced me like one of their own and I appreciated that. They'd given me a shot at being on my own. Sadly, my success with Murder Inc. caused me to finally withdraw from college. My mother was devastated. She thought I wanted to just party and hang out on the set of music videos. Contrary, my life involved so much more. I had a real career.

Real talk.

At that time, Murder Inc. was one of the hottest crews in the industry. It was before all the legal issues and federal investigations. Irv was handling business and everybody was eating. There were also no egos. No one thought they were better than anyone. Drivers were able to sit with artists and interns sat in the CEO's office. It was like everyone had one goal in mind. And that was to make and keep Murder Inc.

successful. I admired that. And even to this day, my relationship with Irv and his brother Chris is good. Unfortunately, that relationship was almost compromised.

One day, I was styling on the set of the "Rain on Me Remix" video. As usual, my work reeked hotness. All the brands I'd chosen for my artist were hot and the styles they loved. I'd gotten into a zone at Murder Inc. and my skills were always on point. That day I had to pull clothes for Ja Rule and Irv Gotti. Sometime after the shoot, I got a call from Ja Rule, someone I least expected. He invited me to a party at his hotel suite. Back then, The Inc. was known for throwing parties in their hotel suites. Although they got wild, it was always a family like atmosphere so I figured this one would be no different. I accepted Ja's invite. A little while later, I got to his suite at the Roni Palace to find no one there but him and his security guard. Now, I'm not naïve by a long shot. And I swear I never rode the short bus, still I stayed. It was obvious that Ja had a *private* party in mind for the two of us.

I should've left right then but I didn't. Even though he played it off in the beginning, giving me lame conversation, I felt uncomfortable. In my mind I kept thinking of excuses to leave but I didn't want to come off rude or snobby. After all, Ja was The Inc's star artist at that time. He had major pull at the label. One bad word from him about me and I could be sent packing. My job meant a lot to me. My foot was finally wedged in the door. He liked how I had been working so far so the goal was for him to recommend me to others. The last thing I wanted to do was shake things up so I just played along with Ja's charade and hoped for the best.

Before that night, I'd never really had a physical attraction to Ja. He wasn't ugly or anything like that to me. I had just never thought about it. But as we were talking, I couldn't help noticing the color of his eyes, the curves of his face, the solid look of his build. When you have a conversation with someone and no one else is around, you tend to notice things like that. There's an intimacy to one-on-one conversations.

Against my better judgment, I ended up staying with him that night. But before that, I told him how I felt about possibly compromising my job situation. I told him I needed my job and the moment had me feeling pressured and uncomfortable. "I don't get down like that," he told me, sincerely. "Winter, we don't have to do it if you don't want to." I spilled my guts even more with reasons why I thought it was a bad idea. "Everything will still be all good," he promised. That all sounded fine but I still didn't trust it. He also informed me he was married, which was a shocker. I had no idea he was locked down. I'd been around him a lot of times but never heard from him or anyone else that he was married.

As I said before, I should've left. I shouldn't have let things go further. But he was Ja Rule, the hottest rapper in the game at that time. Countless women were in love with that raspy voice of his and those thug laced love songs he was flooding the game with. I guess I felt like being with him would be a privilege or something. In the back of my mind, there was also the possibility of losing my job if I didn't go along with the program, despite him assuring me otherwise. I didn't know what to do.

To be honest, sleeping with Ja would probably be far from a disappointment. I knew I would've had to treat it like a booty call. I had to keep it moving and never let it happen. Those were my intentions. I swear they were. But one influential factor made those intentions extremely difficult...

Ja was hung like a damn water hose!

9 Puppet Master

Life seemed to get more exciting by the minute. My adrenaline pumped from the time my feet hit the floor until the time my eyes shut at night. One event after another, I was there, hanging with Hip Hop's finest. Older and slightly wiser, I now felt like I belonged. No longer did I enter a room as someone's date, but now as one of the inner circle. I'd grown more determined, something I'd seen in Jason. He had that same 'work hard, go hard' spirit. Thankfully, through Danny, a mover and shaker in the industry, I'd landed another job styling Drag-On, a Hip Hop artist at Ruff Ryder, and more and more business was being thrown my way. Working with Murder Inc. and Ruff Ryder put me in circles that seemed more like a dream than a reality.

Parading through yet another event more changes stared me in the face. Once again Danny, with his raccoon eyes, presented me with an opportunity that would only add to the highlights headed my way. He managed a few up and coming artist, always had connections and partied frequently. I assume that's why they called him "Disco Danny". Danny introduced me to a guy named TC, who was Cassidy's manager at the time. Cassidy, an up and coming rapper with crazy freestyling skills, had his name buzzing through the industry but he hadn't had any major success at the time. After meeting TC and hearing him say they were looking for a stylist, I jumped at the opportunity. It was my chance to get in from the ground up.

TC informed me that Cassidy had been signed to Full Surface, which was run by his son, Swizz Beatz. Eventually I began to work with Cassidy. I liked his outgoing smooth flair. He was a ladies' man and had a little swag going on so styling him came easy. Plus he came from good stock; somebody had taught him well. His manners were on point, he was very polite, and he knew how to talk to women. We'd do events on a much smaller scale than places my job opportunities had taken me before. There were schools, colleges, and performances at small venues. I even remember him getting booed. But it was a check so I continued, not just with Cassidy but with Murder Inc. as well.

Around that same time I styled Ashanti for *People* Magazine's "Celebs Under 25." I was in my prime: grinding and vowing to make a name for myself in the working world of Hip Hop. I'd walk into the Vivienne Westwood showroom with a letter stating that if anything was damaged the record label took full responsibility and walked back out with over 25 outfits.

It all worked way too easily. I felt like a butterfly gaining its wings. The next six months of my life would turn out to be the craziest ever, and a string of events would prove to change me forever. I would possibly even bear a child from one of Hip Hop's elite.

Early 2003, the word came in. Murder Inc. was heading to Miami for the club opening of their long-time friend, rapper and record producer, Benzino. Club Zinos had been the talk of Miami and the industry. At the time Benzino co-owned *The Source Magazine* and was a hell of a connection so like real good friends do—the Murder Inc. family decided we'd all go support. Right up my alley, the planning wheels turned in motion. Some of the ladies around the office and I decided we'd fly out together and room at the Avalon hotel. Excitement filled me as I thought of what to wear and who would be there. I was on cloud nine. Even though I'd traveled around the country often, there was something about Miami that had my spirits in an uproar.

By the time we made it to the airport we were all in party mode. Lexi, who was signed to Murder Inc. at the time, Sabrina, and Chynae greeted me with hugs. Then I was introduced to Chrissy Lampkin, who is now Jim Jones' girlfriend. Chynae worked for Murder Inc. and Chrissy was her girl who was tagging along for the party. At that time I had no idea we would have so many similarities or that we were cool with some of the same guys. Chrissy's reputation proceeded her. I'd heard a lot about her—good and bad. One, that she was the "it" girl, always fly, never dated broke guys and always had the freshest gear. I was in my early twenties so since she was older I watched her flow. She had her Rolie on, dressed like a million bucks and looked good so instead of hating, I figured…if you can't beat'em, join'em. It was on. We clicked instantly. *Miami wasn't ready for New York babes*, I told myself, ready to party like never before.

The moment we stepped off the plane and into the Miami sun, I felt like something new and vibrant awaited me. Florida always seemed like a place I could call home. I had been countless times, and all were great experiences, except for the one where my mother forced me to see my father.

Walking into that nursing home in Florida annoyed me to the core. At sixteen, I didn't understand why it was so im-

*portant for me to see a man who'd never really served a pur-
pose in my life. And how in the hell did he get sick in
Florida, a place where my light was able to shine? He had
full blown prostate cancer and had moved to Florida with
his siblings so he'd have family around to take care of him.
My mother felt that his condition could worsen and he could
possibly die. She warned me that I would be filled with regret
if I didn't see him face to face. It was my opportunity to tell
him how I felt about him abandoning me and my mom.*

*That all sounded great...real Dr. Phil like. Unfortu-
nately, I didn't have a lot of pity for him. Empathy had never
been a friend to me. I had been that way for too long and he
was partially responsible. He had poured some of the nasty
ingredients into me which made me tick. He helped build the
"Winter" that so many people thought was wild, crazy and
heartless.*

*I walked inside the room and saw him lying in bed. I fi-
nally realized where my nose and chin had come from. His
eyes were light like mine and my facial features resembled
his greatly. I hadn't seen the man in over seven years. Still
there was disgust....a sense of hatred inside. His first words
to me ruined it all.*

"Why did you cut your hair?"

*I looked over my shoulder where my eyes met Jackie's.
I became enraged yet said nothing. This man hadn't seen me
in ages and all he could think to say was some slick comment
about my hair. He'd missed every graduation, every Christmas, my high school prom...and the list goes on. Even
though I knew he was ill and the goal was for us to talk out
our differences, I sat there stone-faced for the rest of the
visit. I didn't say two words to him then and refuse to say two
words to him now. That was unfortunately the last time I saw
my father.*

I drifted back to reality when we pulled up to the hotel.
The Avalon was gorgeous and immediately sent my mind

back into party mode. Chrissy, Chynae, Lexi, Sabrina and I checked into our room and began our weekend extravaganza. We got to the club and realized Benzino's party had to be the party of the year. From the dance floor to the bar, the room was packed and the music played at its highest level—the type of beats that could burst your eardrum. There were plenty women in attendance, but us New York girls got most of the attention. The number of bottles purchased for us seemed insane. I lost count. Benzino had really hooked us up. Dressed scantily in my best, my C cups sat up straight looking as if they'd pop from my all black dress. There wasn't really any female competition. All the competition had come with me from New York. It didn't matter though, there were no guys that I wanted to get with. There had been too much bullshit with niggas by this time in my life.

Everyone important to Murder Inc. showed up including Noreaga and Fat Joe. Of course Irv graced the place. And even Ja Rule showed up. Seeing him always sent me into strategy mode. I assumed he would try to take me back to his hotel by the end of the night, which I would decline again. Since our one and only encounter he'd hinted at hooking up again several times. Each time I declined. I'd grown comfortable in my own skin, not really afraid of losing my job. Besides, he was married and I didn't see him as my lover. So the answer for hooking up was always no- no- and no again. Contrary to what some people may have thought, I'd never been into breaking up happy homes. The advances kept coming....but I do have morals.

That's probably why I wanted to spaz out on Jason when he showed up to the club. Somewhere over the course of the last year he'd switched up on me. In public he would throw me shade like we didn't really know each other the way we did. That night was no different. I saw him from across the room. The music thumped loudly so I didn't expect him to call out my name but a fist pump in the air, puckered lips, a smile or any type of sign of recognition would've worked. He didn't do it and neither did I.

I turned my attention back to my girls who were in straight party mode. The club atmosphere was rocking by this time and the music had gotten good to us. It was noticed that none of 50 Cent or Jay-Z's music played at Club Zino's that night. Their music was needed and missed. At the time Murder Inc. and 50 Cent had a major beef and Jay-Z was on tour with 50 Cent, which meant Benzino wasn't tolerating either artist's music to be played in his club.

While joking about that music issue a fine specimen of a man dressed extremely well walked up to me and introduced himself as one of the Murder Inc. producers, Chink Santana. Once I got wind of his name my heart thundered just a bit. *Beatmaster*, I thought, almost infatuated. His name rang throughout the office and I realized that I had seen him around a lot. We'd never been formally introduced since he was Murder Inc.'s secret weapon. Set-up like a ghost producer, he created the hot beats we all loved from that era. Most people never knew that Chink had put his magic touch on all the big records like "Baby, Baby Baby" and "Thug Lovin'."

All I knew was that he'd gone to school for music, was very talented, had an ego the size of Mount St. Helens, had lots of money and was originally from D.C. I could tell by the way he was dressed that the dollars were rolling in even though he didn't have the popularity of the rest of the family.

As the night progressed, we kicked it for a while in the club, him feeling me and vice versa. He had become my magnet, with me loving his style. His charisma was off the meter. By the end of the night we swapped info. I figured no harm, he was one of us...maybe we'd hook up back in New York. He told me he'd be in Miami for another thirty days. He said he was there to record Ashanti's album.

When I told him I was leaving the next day he asked

me to stay with him.

I couldn't believe those words. But he was real, he didn't want me to leave. He said it so sincerely. Thoughts flipped through my head quickly. Where would I stay? Who from Murder Inc. would find out? Would word get back to Jadakiss? Even though we weren't in a committed relationship I didn't want that. We hadn't been seeing much of each other lately but rumors traveled quickly in the music biz.

I told him, I had to go home to make money, letting my tone make him understand that if I missed money by staying with him he'd have to replace it. He assured me real sexy like that he had me, so I stayed.

I told him I was a stylist. But none of that mattered to Chink. He put the pressure on me; heavy pressure, executing all of his smooth talking skills. The attraction to me seemed strong. He damn near begged. *Here we go with this music industry shit*, I told myself. But when he promised to send me home if I didn't like staying with him that was the last straw. "I'll put you on a plane whenever you're ready to go home," Chink ended. For some crazy reason I agreed.

My new Miami life consisted of mini-mansion type living. Waking up to champagne, exquisite food, and good sex—it all had me in la la land like the grind was over. Just imagine waking up and able to go for a swim in your backyard that was adjacent to the beach. Nothing like it! I'd been accustomed to spending my days scouting out the next styling gig for some record label. I always had to hop in New York City cabs or pay ridiculous parking prices just to make moves in New York. Now I slept with the producer who created most of Murder Inc.'s hits in a fabulous house in Miami. That was the life!

We shopped constantly marching through the Bal Harbour Shops. And since I moved in with Chink with literally the bag I'd left New York with, new clothes were needed daily. He bought it all, no questions asked—Neiman Marcus, Saks Fifth Avenue, and every store Miami had to offer. It seemed like a fairy tale until the real Chink made an appearance. It's crazy how something can look so good on the outside but be real foul on the inside. It didn't take me long to realize Chink had come from nothing and the world of Hip Hop and his celebrity status had affected him in a negative way. Others had warned me that Chink was a womanizer. Soon, I got a whiff of it. He talked down to everyone around us, often times trying me too. But my mouth was fire…ready to pounce back on him when he tried. Somehow he felt entitled like everything had to go his way. Everybody was a 'bitch' to him. Bitch this and bitch that! He used the word like a pronoun, dishing it out every chance he got. It turned into a level of disrespect I hadn't experienced with Murder Inc. Although Ja Rule had his flings, he was totally respectful, always considerate of others so since they came from the same culture and climate I expected the same from Chink. Nah! His ego was insane.

By my second week at the house he had invited other women to the house, ones he had sexual relationships with. Thank God I made his ass use condoms each and every time. Catching something was my worse fear. I hadn't become emotionally tied to him, so for me, it was no sweat. I understood where we were going….nowhere…yet the money and good living still flowed. I figured where else would I go and have a lavish lifestyle that someone else paid for. I mean where else would I go where Ashanti lived in the mansion next door?

Before long, it was time for me to go. My intuition told me that would be the end of me and Chink. He had enough women on his little string that I figured he wouldn't even remember my name by Christmas. Before leaving I told him I would be at my grandmother's house in Brooklyn and that he could hit me up once he got to the city. That's when his next proposition arose.

He offered to let me stay in his apartment in New Jersey for free.

I could stay rent free? Aw hell! Another bell went off. I should've known not to accept....but I did. Free rent and a chance to get out of the projects was all I needed to hear. So I left Miami, went back to Brooklyn and soon found myself living in an apartment in New Jersey where Chink Santana footed the bills. Unbeknownst to me, someone else lived there too. It wasn't just me.

Games! Always games.

10   <u>Trust No Man</u>

Games. Trust me, in this industry, everyone plays them. Either you're the player or you're getting played. You use or you get used. It's not personal. That's just the way it is. And the quicker you realize it, the better off you'll be. I'd realized it, accepted it and I was using it to my advantage. That's why the arrangement I had with Chink Santana worked for me.

Our relationship wasn't going anywhere. That was more than obvious. But rather than walk away, I continued to stay at the spot in New Jersey with him and his assistant. Shit, he was still paying the rent and bills so why not? Like I said, you use or you get used. Chink rarely stopped by the spot. When he did, it was usually for some ass. Most of the time, he was at the studio or taking care of his business affairs for Murder Inc. Other times, he was at home with his baby's momma who lived only two blocks away. By this time, it didn't bother me, my feelings didn't come into play. He was serving a purpose and I'd gotten the memo on his juggling act. He snored like a grizzly bear anyway so he did me a favor. It was crazy how he'd bring other girls or "friends" to the apartment where I lay my head. Even though

85

I didn't care, that was downright rude.

One night in particular he waltzed into the bedroom where we both slept whenever he came through. After tapping me on the shoulder he allowed the most asinine words to come from his mouth.

"Go sleep on the couch."

That shit was historic! He had balls. I turned to see a woman standing behind him. "Whatever nigga," I said, while grabbing my blanket and hauling ass toward the couch.

But Chink's antics didn't bother me because I was getting used to the game. One day, Janine and I were out on 57th & Broadway when we saw a yellow Lambo getting towed. Obviously, the sight drew attention. Janine and I went over to investigate, figuring the owner was probably someone famous. Come to find out, it was. The owner was Swizz Beatz. *Bingo*, I told myself. He introduced himself to Janine and me like he knew us. He didn't seem to be stuck on himself. I liked that. He even told us why his car was being towed. He said he was having it shipped out of New York.

After our small talk, I got his number.

Now I knew exactly who Swizz Beatz was. I knew he was a producer and I knew he had his own company, Full Surface. But most importantly, I knew he was married. I had no intention of being a home wrecker. Just like Chink, I was merely hoping to use Swizz to serve a purpose. You know, maybe get a few vacations and high priced bags out of him. In the beginning, that's exactly how things went between us. We'd eat at fancy restaurants late at night after he finished at the studio or meet up somewhere discreet just to spend a little time with one another. Swizz was one of those arrogant, inconsiderate brothers who thinks the world revolves around him so he always told me when and where to meet him. Most times it was somewhere secluded, away from wandering eyes.

Our relationship grew quickly the moment we 'got it

in' for the first time. Of course, Swizz kept us a secret. Since he was married, it was self-explanatory. He also didn't really want the industry in his business. He preferred to keep everything *about* us *between* us, which was all good with me. So it came as no surprise that we'd meet in the most unlikely places. The Full Surface office is where I first got christened and realized he was the biggest I'd ever had. Table top, on the desk, he punished the pussy amongst the many music related plaques that lined the wall. Posters of his first son and even a portrait of him and Mashonda had its place on the wall too. *How disrespectful*, I thought. Every time my eyes peered at Mashonda's oversized portrait on the wall I felt like she was putting a hex on me.

He treated me like it was the best he'd ever had re-questing more as soon as each session ended. I was flattered so when he called me just a few weeks later and asked me to meet him not far from the studio I agreed. The moment our eyes connected I knew what it was. "Let me get some," he commented. I kept thinking maybe we'd go to a hotel but no….he meant right then. Next thing I knew we were in the back seat of my car with him on top of me giving me swollen lips once again. Sometimes I would literally be in pain after fucking him. I mean I could feel my uterus tilting often when we were done, and I was barely able to walk.

That went on for a while, wild sexcapades and spo-radic meetings. Swizz was crafty like that. At the time, of course, Chink would still ring my phone from time to time, thinking he owned me just because he paid the bills at the spot. But shit, obviously he was doing his thing so I saw nothing wrong with doing mine. I had even hooked up with Jadakiss again despite the way he was throwing me shade in front of people. A part of my heart was still his but I wasn't interested in trying to truly rekindle what we once had. I just liked being around him because of our history together.

Every woman has that one man in her life who no matter how much she wants to forget him, she can't. For me, Jason was that man. But Swizz and Chink were each like credit cards that I used when nothing else was available. Nothing personal. But I'd learned that it was always best to keep more than one man on hand because you never know when you might need a Gucci bag, a piece of jewelry, or a bill paid. I'd also grown pretty good at juggling niggas and keeping it quiet. I'd picked it up from Dame.

Swizz was cool and because he had major paper we could hit up a lot of places. He spoiled me and spent a lot of time with me. The only thing I didn't quite like was his sexual habits. Swizz didn't like to use condoms at all. That didn't sit too well with me. It had me thinking, if he was fucking me with no protection, who else was he fucking with no protection? I wasn't feeling that at all. The last thing I wanted to do was take a chance on catching AIDS or getting pregnant. I wasn't ready to die and I wasn't ready for kids so I insisted he use a condom. He tried to talk me out of it of course.

Swizz and I began to spend more time together. Cassidy had gotten busy so Swizz and I became workmates often, keeping our relationship professional in front of others. Besides, Swizz had made it absolutely clear to me from the jump that he would *never* leave his wife under any circumstances. She would always be first in his life. For that, I respected him. He did everything he could to keep her protected and us a secret. That's why I don't quite understand why he did what he did one particular night.

We were out at a restaurant grabbing something to eat after the club. We were sitting at a table when Cassidy's boy Niko tried to holla at me. For some reason, as Niko continued to get at me, Swizz started acting strange. I mean, it was like he was getting jealous and it was obvious. He even kept bumping my leg underneath the table. Finally out of nowhere, he announced to Niko that I was his woman. The shit shocked the hell out of me more than everyone else.

In all honesty, when he put it out there, the first thing I thought about was his wife, Mashonda. By him admitting to everyone the reality about us, I knew there was a chance it would get back to his wife. After all this time of trying to keep her protected, I wondered why he would take a chance on jeopardizing their relationship.

Mashonda was around often. She was always showing support for him. Each time they were out, Swizz treated her like she was the most important woman in the room. I stayed in my lane. I knew my position and played it well, even when she and I worked on set during one of Cassidy's videos. I worked just as hard to keep us a secret as he did so it just didn't make any sense to me as to why he put us out there.

Swizz was already starting to skate on thin ice with Mashonda just before the night at the club. I'd actually witnessed an argument between them while riding in the SUV headed to Philly for Cassidy's show when Swizz's phone rang. I knew he would answer; he always answered her calls. As soon as he picked up, she spazzed out on him, accusing him of fucking the R&B singer, Mya. I remained silent, ear hustling. When he finally hung up, I asked him if he'd been fucking Mya. I wanted to know since he'd been treating me like Mashonda and I were the only two women in his life. He didn't answer. He just had that Simple Simon look on his face that I've seen a million times before when men get busted. I stayed with him though. And his demands grew stronger, his sexual appetite too.

Once I thought we were just hanging out and eating after leaving the studio. I had my feet on the dash of his Range Rover chilling when Swizz made yet another spontaneous proposition. "Let's find a spot," he said smoothly. The shit just rolled off of his tongue. My facial expression warned him that something was wrong. After he tried to figure out what the problem was, I finally told him, "I'm on." He kept driving until he pulled over to what I considered the most romantic spot you'd want to find to fuck in the car. A compact spot overlooking New York City. I knew what it was and warding him off would be hard. Swizz always got what he wanted. Before long, he grabbed some sort of t-shirt or towel. It didn't take long for him to enter me with his thickness once again.

When I look back on the whole Swizz and me thing, I do feel terrible. Mashonda will never believe that, but it really is the truth. When a woman holds her man down the way she held Swizz down, she should be rewarded with that man's loyalty. She deserves it.

I was immature and blinded by someone else's fame and only thinking about myself during that situation. But in all actuality, when Mashonda looks at the eventual break up of their marriage, she has to admit that it wasn't me who actually broke up her marriage, now was it? Not trying to be a smart ass. It just is what it is.

Still, our escapades continued.

11 Never Bite The Hand That Feeds You

When I heard that I would be heading to Arizona to meet Swizz a sensual feeling came over me. This escapade differed from the others. He and Mashonda were already in Arizona and I'd be flying in as she was flying out. When I first heard the sketchy details a part of me knew it was wrong to go. Against my better judgment, I flew out anyway. By the time I landed and Swizz picked me up in a sky blue Aston Martin, I got hyped about our time together in the dry state. I'd never been to Arizona before and had tons of questions for Swizz but his silence told me something shady was going on. His weird mannerisms gave me all the signs. I knew him well by then. We'd been messing around for roughly two months.

"So, what's up? What are we doing?" I asked eagerly.

He still gave me that shady, up to no good look. "Swizz, what's up?" I asked him again.

When his words finally flew from his lips I wanted to punch him in the face.

He actually said he didn't want to do anything while Mashonda's in the air.

"She hasn't called me yet," he uttered.

"And?" I spat sarcastically.

He didn't respond. He simply drove to the Sanctuary Hotel where he and Mashonda had a luxurious suite. Once inside, he still didn't say much while waiting for her call. Her flight should've landed a while before we made it back into the room. It didn't and soon Swizz began to panic. He thought Mashonda might've been slick enough to show up at the room to catch him with me. He began rubbing his head, pacing the floor and talking real crazy, dialing her number back to back. At that point I'd become irritated with the start of my trip.

The next thing I knew he'd gotten another room across the hall and moved my stuff into that room. He was crafty like that; always staying ahead of the game when he cheated. We didn't even have sex while he waited for her call. Mashonda had his mind gone, or maybe that was just a guilty conscience. Finally, hours later, she called. The conversation was brief. I remember him saying, "I'm about to go to the studio."

Not sure what she said but just like that he hung up and transformed into the Swizz I knew. "We can go back into the other room now," he instructed. As usual we had wild, crazy sex and we shopped, this time the Louis Vuitton store, my favorite. There were dinners every night including one of my favorites, P.F. Changs. I should've felt guilty about sleeping with Swizz...maybe that's why karma caught up with me sooner than I thought. As soon as I got back to Jersey some bullshit was thrown in my face.

Gossip, such a terrible thing.

Word had gotten back to Chink about me and Ja. Although Irv and I are still good these days and I'm thankful to him for allowing me to be a part of Murder Inc., either Irv or his brother Chris dry snitched on me about sleeping with Ja. Chink wouldn't say which one. I was pissed at Ja, too for not keeping what we did between us. We simply spent a night together. But men will be men, I guess. They gossip just like broads no matter what they want the rest of the world to believe.

When Chink got word about the Ja situation, obviously he was angry. The moment we saw each other when I returned from Arizona it all began. He saw all my bags, compliments of Swizz, and shouted when his eyes spotted the Louis Vuitton bag, "Where that shit come from?"

"A styling job with DMX." The lie rolled off my tongue so effortlessly. I really had pulled clothes for DMX just not when I said I did.

He pulled me out the apartment and said, "We gotta talk."

We walked outside so nobody else would hear our business. "Why didn't you tell me?" he said. I denied the shit with a straight face and puppy dog eyes but it didn't do any good. "Yo, Winter, I know, Irv told me."

"Rumors are always being spread and niggas never know what they're talking about," I shouted. Obviously, he never spoke to Rule. I know he wouldn't have lied on me.

"The shit's embarrassing!"

His tone had gotten too high. Had he forgotten I wasn't his chick? Had he forgotten he'd brought other chicks around me and paraded them in my face? That payback shit hurts…sometimes.

"You got me looking stupid," he added tugging at my shirt and moving way too close to my face.

At that moment I knew he wouldn't be able to get past the Ja situation.

My thoughts spiraled. The nerve, nigga. You live with your bitch up the street and everyone knows it, but you're embarrassed? No, your ego is embarrassed.

"If you want me to leave, I will," I finally stated.

"Yeah. I do," he said firmly.

That's when my meal ticket with Chink was cut and I was handed my walking papers. I packed up that same day and he quit messing with me. Period. There was no more free rent, food and money. Gloom filled me for a moment. There's no sense in lying. But after realizing how average the sex was and that I never truly had real feelings for him, I decided to keep it moving. Besides, it wasn't like I really needed him. My styling career had taken off enough to keep money in my pocket and me on my feet. What I was getting from him was just a bonus. My mentality was always that *I would get over it.*

After moving out of Chink's spot, I moved back in with my grandmother in the projects. Even though I was getting money I thought it was best to save it, not knowing how many of my other sponsors would come through. Looking back on it now, obviously the move was immature. I should've gotten my own place. I guess deep down inside I was scared to stand on my own. Something inside me had me feeling like I needed someone else to foot the bills; they were my safety net. It was childish, I realize now. Back then, though, that was just the way I did things.

Moving in with my grandmother was a bad look. I'd downgraded. Here I was, under the arms of big name rappers, attending big name events and styling for good money. But I had been reduced to having to move back into the projects like Florence Ballard of The Supremes. It seemed crazy to other people but I didn't see it that way. I'd always been close to the hood. I still am, to be honest. Although my body may leave the hood, my heart never will. I guess that's one of the main reasons why I didn't see a problem with it.

Just a few weeks later more drama headed my way. It came in the form of a damn snake who was supposed to be my friend. But since what Swizz and I had was built on deceit, I guess I deserved it. The end started when Danny did some bullshit. At that time, despite knowing Swizz was possibly sleeping with Mya and Lord knows whoever else, I'd begun to fall back from Jadakiss. Chances of me getting caught became too frequent. I would even avoid going to studio sessions or industry events if I knew there was even the possibility of running into Jada while with Swizz. Since it was now out there that Swizz and I were together, one day I asked Danny for some advice regarding Swizz. Little did I know where the conversation would lead. During our talk, he mentioned that everyone who knew Swizz knew that he didn't like to wear a condom. That surprised me. I had no idea Swizz discussed something that personal with people. Anyway, Danny jokingly said I should get knocked up by Swizz and let one of the child support payments buy him a Range Rover similar to the one Swizz drove. I laughed it off.

A few days later, Swizz wasn't answering my calls. It was weird. We normally talked three to four times a day. Eventually, I figured he'd gotten interested in someone else. But I didn't care at that point, I wasn't trying to play his games. Besides, my uterus needed a break anyway.

I ended up seeing him the next day when Danny called and told me to pick up my check from him in Yonkers at the Ruff Ryders studio. I got there and saw Swizz. It was an eerie feeling. I should've known something was up from the cunning look in Danny's eyes. Swizz didn't speak. So, I didn't speak either. It all seemed childish to me. But as soon as I left the studio, Swizz called and told me to meet him up the street at the McDonalds.

When he pulled up in his Mercedes Benz wagon I could tell from his facial expression he had an issue with me. Come to find out, Danny did some real live hoe shit that I would have never expected from him. He'd told Swizz about our conversation but put a spin on it by saying that I told him I was going to get pregnant by him purposely and celebrate by buying myself a brand new Range Rover with Swizz's *money.* I couldn't believe that shit.

But obviously Swizz did at first. That's why he hadn't been answering any of my calls. At first we argued about it. I stepped to him hard, letting him know my feelings. "You putting me through too much grief for someone who's married." I hit him with my signature finger popping, moving up and down and neck swirling. I couldn't believe he fed into something so childish. Eventually, he admitted that he'd spoken to his Uncle Dee who knew Danny very well. He told me that his uncle had gotten at him about believing Danny. He told Swizz that Danny had lied. Everything looked like it was going to get back on track for us.

The very next day I lit into Danny's ass. It pissed me off so bad. "You fuckin' snake in the grass," I began. "Why would you do some foul shit like that!"

He lied from the moment words flew from his mouth. As I told him everything Swizz told me that he said, he denied all of that too. I didn't believe Danny one bit but he helped to feed my hustle. We were still sorta like business partners. He'd gotten me the Drag-On and Cassidy jobs. We were getting money together making $1500 per job, styling for video shoots, magazine covers, album packaging and much more. That fact rose above everything else. I was making that money on my own and more opportunities through Danny would come. I couldn't jeopardize that, especially now that Swizz and I weren't one hundred percent.

But once again, because of Danny, shit between me and Swizz ended; this time, for good.

Swizz didn't like me remaining cool with Danny after what Danny had done. I understood but Danny was my bread and butter. I didn't have the stability Swizz had so I couldn't take a chance on getting left out there. I had to fuck with him. Swizz didn't want to understand that though. It all came to a head a few days later during the Bang Bang Boom video shoot in Miami for Drag-On's new song which featured

Swizz.

Danny and I were having a harmless conversation. He said something that made me laugh. All of a sudden, Swizz stormed over to us and went off on me in front of everyone. "You real foul, embarrassing me in front of Danny," he shouted. "And you over here talking about me."

I tried to explain that we weren't discussing him at all and that he was being childish but his last words sent my blood boiling. "And you should've been more discreet about our relationship."

"Really?" was all I could say, but in my head all sorts of thoughts swirled around. He was the one who decided to let everyone know about our fling. I never went around boasting or bragging. Our relationship was over for good at that point. Our many months together had ended. The shit hurt. I won't lie and say that it didn't. It seemed like the older I got the softer I had become. But in true Winter fashion, I had no choice but to snap back and keep it moving, understanding that jump-offs come and go. Mine was now gone.

His phone calls stopped. His visits stopped. There were no more dates, no more sex, no more anything.

Strangely though, my first thought was to find Jason.

12 _____ Jetsetting

Time moved swiftly after Swizz, yet my life didn't slow down. I went straight into party mode.

Refusing to miss a beat, I did what I know: I snatched up another dude with deep pockets and worked my magic. His name was Tye and I had him so gone he took me on a vacation to Cancun for the annual Memorial Day celebration. It was like Freaknic in Atlanta. There were black folks everywhere. Attending wasn't new to me though. I'd been many times before with my girls.

There was always a wide variety of men there. You had regular hardworking dudes who had to save heavy to attend. You had drug dealers and pimps. You had doctors and lawyers. You had rappers, celebrities and athletes. Whatever a woman wanted or needed in a man, it was there. My only problem this year was I'd taken sand to the beach. I was there with Tye so of course that complicated shit for me and cramped my style.

Don't get me wrong. I liked Tye. He wasn't a celebrity but that was cool with me. I was trying to take a break from that shit and see if there was quite possibly something else out there for me on the relationship side. I was tired of the bullshit and disappointments I kept going through with rappers. That was for the birds. I wanted to see if things could be different with Tye. But there was a problem. As Jay-Z said, "When a good girl's gone bad, she's gone forever." I'd been hurt and betrayed so many times before that each *past* man made it worse for the *next* man. So although Tye was cool people and had never done anything to make me betray him, I was already so set in my ways that I didn't know how to be the faithful woman he deserved. Because of that, the vacation pretty much sealed the end for us. We just didn't know it yet.

While on the trip, I spotted a group of guys all rocking Tees with various catchy slogans, which also had the letters BMF. They were obviously not from NY since I'd never seen them before. Surely my claws would've gotten to them already. They smelled bossy, fa real. You could recognize it. Their swagger just exuded the shit. They were all young, thuggish, spending money like it was going out of style and buying up so many bottles of liquor and champagne that there was barely enough for everyone else. I mean, these niggas were *really* going hard. I was intrigued. And so were the other patrons of the club since the DJ kept announcing the shit.

Although each of them dressed in black and white Tees, one guy in particular who was surrounded by dozens of other young players, sent someone to ask me if I wanted to take a picture. I couldn't help myself. We eventually got introduced, took the picture and spat a few words to one another. He told me he and his crew were in the music business, they were BMF, Black Mafia Family and that his name was Blue. That was strange to me. I'd been around for a minute and had never heard of BMF.

We talked for a few more moments then I got his number and fell back. Since I was there with Tye and his friends I didn't want to be outright disrespectful. I knew all eyes were on me. Still though, after parting ways with him, he and the letters BMF stayed on my mind.

A few days after heading back to New York, as luck would have it, I saw a few of the same BMF guys at another club. They were once again dressed in black and white like they were their official colors or something. Something was definitely up with these dudes, I realized. They were obviously making moves and I wanted to know what those moves were. Just like in Cancun, these cats were buying out the *entire* bar. The shit was crazy. I'd been around hustlers, rappers and music execs. But most of them, although caked up, didn't have enough money to buy the bar out.

I smelled a baller.

Stayed curious as hell.

I watched from afar until one of the mystery men approached me and sparked up a conversation. This time I had to get more info on them than I had back in Cancun. This time, instead of just exchanging numbers, me and this dude had a detailed conversation. He told me his name was Baby Blue and he was from L.A. I assumed he was the same guy from Cancun so I said, "We met in Cancun a few days ago, right?"

"Yeah, we did," he replied.

Since I knew BMF was in the music biz, I figured that was his stage name. As we talked, I was feeling his vibe hard. I mean, his swag was off the chain. We connected so quickly that somewhere between that night and the next morning he invited me to Atlanta and I accepted.

Of course, it was silly to just up and leave for Atlanta with a nigga I didn't know. These days, I'd call a broad a bird brain for it. But back then, life was one big party for me. I didn't think about tomorrow or consequences. That type of stuff never crossed my mind. All I knew was this baller had fat pockets and he wanted to fuck with a woman like me. That's what I was focused on. I figured a few days in the

ATL wouldn't hurt me. Besides, what were the chances of us meeting again in NY a few days later? I felt it was meant to be.

The great thing about being young, especially in the position I was in, is that there weren't many household tasks, big bills to pay; nor did I have any kids. I wasn't married and didn't think a husband would come any time soon. Basically, I had nothing to hold me back or tie me down so I was free to just up and bounce whenever I wanted. Also, since I had no responsibilities, the money I was making styling went directly into my pocket. I didn't have to break bread with anyone. That was great because my styling career was growing. I was now doing work for Ruff Ryder, Full Surface, Murder Inc. and few others on a regular basis. Life seemed good.

So, I headed to the airport the next day anxious to see what my new connection had to offer. At the gate, I walked up to the guy I thought I was there to meet when another guy with similar looks called out to me. I was surprised to discover that the guy I'd met in Cancun was actually Blue, Baby Blue's older brother. They all made jokes about the mix-up but instantly made me choose. It was cool though, I understood. I ended up with the little brother, Baby Blue. That was a good move since on the flight it was discovered that Blue was a rapper and they were going to be filming a video in Atlanta. At least for once I wasn't caught up with a rapper. Through more conversation I told them about my styling jobs with Murder Inc. which sparked major interest with Blue. He immediately told me I could style him for the video and would be paid sizably. The idea of mixing business with pleasure was music to my ears. My networking was now making sense.

The moment we landed and drove through the city I was struck by something that would eventually become an important part of my life. We were riding in the Suburban when a song came over the radio. I liked it as soon as I heard it. Nodding my head to it, I asked, "Who is this?" Baby Blue didn't answer. He just ignored me. There were about five or six people riding, they didn't answer me either. In the silence, I realized I probably sounded like a groupie so I let it go. But in my mind, something about that voice on the song had me hooked. Its sound and tone was unique. It filled me. Sorta had me wet. I'd never heard a voice like it. I wanted to meet whoever was behind it. Someday I would but left it alone for the time.

That same day Baby Blue took me out to Justin's, Puffy's spot, with his crew. Blue had actually rented the place for a private party with their own DJ, open bar, and private chef cooking for about a hundred people. Immediately, he and his dudes began running through money like water. The shit was surreal. It was like money was nothing to them.

Justin's was filled with people rockin' jewelry and wearing expensive clothes. Obviously, they were movers and shakers in their own right. I mingled with some of them and was surprised to see a familiar face. It was Fabolous. I was happy to see him but he wasn't feeling the same way. He gave me the disapproving look that I'd grow to know and recognize so well.

"What the hell are you doing here?" he asked.

"Chillin'," I told him.

Fab was with his brother Cain and good friend Shaq who seemed more happy to see me. I hugged both Shaq and Cain and eventually took a picture with Fabolous.

He seemed concerned that I was hanging out with a bunch of guys. "Winter, you shouldn't be here." Maybe he knew something I didn't know or perhaps he was just jealous.

I shrugged it off and told him I was good. I figured I could handle myself no matter what.

Eventually, I left Fab and went on about my business. I had no idea that he was there to do the video with Blue.

Later that evening, Baby Blue took me back to the house he and his crew shared. The nigga wasn't frontin'. My mouth dropped at the sight of his crib. It was a six bedroom house with marble floors, granite counter tops, iron staircases, walk in closets, multiple bathrooms and a whole bunch of other expensive bells and whistles. At that moment, I knew I was going to be in Atlanta for more than just a few days.

The Swissotel, as it was called back then, became our home. And although my bags and toiletries remained at the hotel, most days were spent at the main house. Every day was the same enjoyable routine: partying, clubbing, shopping sprees, riding in Lambos, smoking the best weed, drinking the best champagne and so much more. We did all that from morning 'till night, most of the time until the sun came up again. It was nothing to Baby Blue and his BMF crew. It was pretty much their lifestyle and they never deviated from it. If they didn't do it big, they didn't see the need in doing it at all. I loved just hanging out with them.

Each night was topped off with sex and plenty of it. Although I liked sex with Baby Blue it wasn't all I'd expected. It was nowhere near as dazzling as his lifestyle. He wasn't as long and thick as his money. His sex game was boring and predictable...but he treated me like I was really his girl. For that, I respected him a lot. Early on he told me he loved me and waited for me to say it back.

I never did.

I'd never even said it to Smiley.

Besides in my head, I thought, *Damn, I just met you, why would I love you? Let's stop talking about love and let's head to the mall.*

Still, in his head, I know he thought I was his girl. And he protected me like a man would protect his woman. During our make-out sessions he'd act real affectionate, kissing, hugging, pulling me close. Still in all, I knew what it was.

With everything that was going on, some days I realized I was losing focus on what I was supposed to be focused on... my career. Calls for jobs weren't coming since I'd gotten to Atlanta but I was having so much fun that I never even thought to find out why. I wasn't even promoting myself anymore, knowing that more money awaited me if I'd booked a few more jobs. I'd gotten paid ten grand just for styling Blue for the video he Fab and E40 did together. Despite that, the parties and gatherings the BMF crew was treating me to overshadowed it all. I was more blinded by the lights than ever before. Besides, Baby Blue was showing me off to others like I was definitely his.

During that time, he and his crew booked thirty rooms at The Swissotel one weekend and flew five of my friends in from New York to consummate the weekend. That was the type of shit they did. They never planned for anything. They were always spontaneous. When something popped into their mind, they just *did* it with no worries about how much it would cost. If they saw a Maserati or Ferarri on the lot, they bought it right then and there. If they saw a house they wanted, they bought it right then and there. I mean, money was never a problem. No one I had ever been around did it like that. No one!

Anyway, it was around this time that I saw Mimi again, who we now know as a member of the Stevie J love triangle on Love and Hip Hop Atlanta. It was good seeing a familiar face since I'd seen her around Ja Rule a few times. Mimi had her own cleaning company and it was nothing for members of BMF to have maids and chefs in their homes. Mimi used to cook and clean for them. Sometimes she was there to cook and clean and sometimes she was spending the night. I would often help her cook, or just hang out in the living room together drinking champagne or just having girl talk. It was good having a comrade in the house, someone that I knew, making me feel more comfortable.

Enjoyable times rarely last forever, or at least not without something coming along and knocking you on your ass. I'm not special so I'm no exception to that rule. My reality check came about four weeks later. As usual, Baby Blue, his homies and I were out at a club getting it in. Out of nowhere, I got sick and couldn't figure out why. I was weak and throwing up. It was crazy. I'd never experienced a feeling like it and for days it didn't seem to want to let up. At first, I thought it was food poisoning. Eventually, I finally figured out what was up. It *definitely* wasn't food poisoning.

Come to find out I was pregnant.

I went into a panic. I wasn't ready for a child. Lord knows I wasn't. I was also ashamed; so ashamed that I didn't want to tell anyone. I didn't want anyone to know. All I knew was that I had used condoms in *all* of my recent sexual experiences. Had someone tricked me? I'd heard about people punching holes in condoms.

It became a difficult and emotional situation for me. For a long time, I dwelled on what to do. I was lost and scared. For the longest, I'd always thought I was a woman. I'd always thought I was grown. I thought I'd faced every problem a woman could face so I could handle anything. This, though, knocked me down a few pegs. It let me know that there was still so much to learn about being a woman. I was still a child scared to grow up.

I'm not perfect. I never was and never will be. I was *then* and still am *now* a work in progress. Because of that, I made a decision that I will always regret.

Rosana and Tina a few older friends of mine were with me when I got it done back in New York. They knew me having a baby wasn't a good idea. I was scared and it took some serious thinking to make the final decision. I thought about me never being able to have children down the line if there were complications. I prayed on it and at the time thought I made the right decision. But I know now that God has a plan and I put it in his hands then and now. I can't question his plan for me. I knew the importance of using condoms and was using protection so it wasn't me being irresponsible. For that part, I didn't feel guilty. I saw it as a mistake and I had to do what was best for myself and my unborn child.

With that said, to all those reading this and frowning down at me on your Mother Teresa thing, don't judge me unless you've never sinned a day in your life.

13   Puerto Rico

More time passed. More parties passed too. Not long after leaving Atlanta the realization came that I'd been on the run for eight years just having fun. It was 2004 and I'd been partying since 1996. I fell back just slightly…slowed down just a bit. After pretending to be married to Baby Blue for 30 days while living in Atlanta I had to do some soul searching. The BMF environment had gotten really wild. I needed a change. I had promised myself to think more clearly before getting deeply involved with another man. I still kept Baby Blue on my injured reserve list.

I found myself in the studio with Cassidy. "Hotel" by Cassidy, his debut single that he'd done with R. Kelly, had turned out to be a certified banger. The video was all over television and the song itself was especially getting love in the clubs. Everyone was in love with it. Its huge success had his label keeping him busy in the studio working on his debut album Split Personality, as well as doing interviews, photo sessions and everything under the sun for promotion. He was their Million Dollar Kid and of course I was right there along for the ride.

Not only did I style for him but we became cool. We really grew close. And once again, it was just like the Jason situation. I was getting a chance to see the appreciative side of a rapper, the innocent side before the game took him over like it had done to so many others. It was fun. We hung out a lot. He treated me like a sister and I treated him like a brother.

Despite me and Swizz no longer fuckin' around anymore, the two of us continued to remain cordial. From him I'd learned the valuable lesson that just because you were mad at someone you did business with, it didn't mean that you couldn't put it aside and still get money with them. Never fuck up your money over personal squabbles. But because he'd put the word out that one time, everyone assumed we were still fucking. They figured we *had* to be. But they were wrong. When Swizz exploded on me at that video shoot in front of everyone and said he wasn't fuckin' with me anymore, he meant it. Well at least, sexually. But as I said, we still remained cool as far as business was concerned.

One night, we were hanging at the studio. It was Cassidy, myself and some broad he had flown in from London to chill with him. Cassidy was in and out of the booth that night putting the finishing touches on what would be his platinum debut while Swizz aggressively manned the boards, making sure the release would be hot. As the music thumped loudly, the entire studio was cloudy with weed smoke. We were each keeping a blunt in constant rotation, excluding Swizz. It was always like that during most of the recording sessions I sat in. Rappers and producers couldn't seem to function unless they had no less than a pound of weed on deck. That was what always seemed to get their creative juices flowing. There was also always plenty of liquor. Cassidy's session was no different.

The most ironic part about that session was how no matter what, Swizz always handled business. He showed there were no hard feelings between us when he asked me to get on the skit which ended up being the intro to the Hotel Remix that Cassidy did with R. Kelly and Trina. I had no bad feelings toward him either so I did it.

As we blazed, drank, and nodded our heads to the music, out of nowhere Cassidy asked me to fly out with him and his crew to Puerto Rico the next day. They were going for a conference. It caught me off guard. He hadn't mentioned anything about the trip to Puerto Rico before that moment. I didn't have any clothes ready, wouldn't even consider paying for my own plane ticket and had no date to bun up with at night.

"You payin' my way?" I asked.

"I got you," he said.

It didn't take long for me to decide. I was used to jet-setting from city to city and after just coming off the ride of my life with Baby Blue my taste buds were ready for a little fun. Just like that I'd forgotten about all my reflections. My life was crazy like that. Before I knew it, we were sitting in first class on a plane sipping champagne headed out to sun filled Puerto Rico. Although I'd gotten to see many different places courtesy of my connections in the industry, none excited me more than getting the chance to go to Puerto Rico. It was my native land. It was where my people had come from. I hadn't been that excited about going to a specific place since the day Smiley told me he was taking me to Vegas.

My grandmother had told me millions of stories about Puerto Rico. She'd always told me how beautiful it was. But despite what she'd said, there was no substitute for experiencing it myself. From the moment I stepped off the plane, I was in love. It was much more than how I'd heard or imagined it would be.

The label had booked us in a plush hotel filled with villas and cottages. That was definitely new to me. I'd never

known there were hotels designed that way. I was used to
floors and suites. It was all good though. The only fucked up
thing about it was I would have to share a room with Cassidy's assistant and a few others. That was definitely a turn
off. It reminded me of my dorm back at college but what else
could I do other than come out my own pocket? Swizz was
footing the bill on Cassidy's stay. And he and I weren't getting it in anymore. Also, I didn't have a consistent sponsor in
my life at that time. I had called it quits with Baby Blue and
me and Jason weren't steady. On my own, my funds were
low at that time so the last thing I could do was complain.
Besides, how many people were getting an all-expense paid
trip to Puerto Rico? How often does that happen? How could
I complain about that?

The DJ conference we were there to attend was a monster. It was huge. Nearly all the movers and shakers in Hip
Hop were there. When we reached the lobby, there was nothing but laughter, loud talking, and wall to wall dudes. I recognized faces immediately. Puffy and his Bad Boy crew
were there. Kanye West and Keyshia Cole were there. Snoop
was also there. Of course, I had been a "Chronic" fan and
"Doggy Style" fan like nearly everyone else in Hip Hop so I
was excited to see him standing that close to me.

Without exaggeration, there were at least a thousand
bodies in that lobby. Every rapper had a crew on top of security. They also had assistants who themselves had assistants.
It was wild. It also came off like a reunion as each rapper
conversed with one another about the last time they'd connected. They talked about females they'd fucked, places
they'd been, award shows they'd attended, niggas they'd
smacked up, weed they'd smoked and a whole lot more.

As time passed, everyone began to check into their
rooms. Through all the commotion, I noticed Jason. I'm not
going to lie about it. I'd really missed him, the real him. And
at that point I had decided if he attempted to play me by 'not

speaking to me in public' there would be hell to pay. I just wasn't going for it.

When I saw his smile, it melted me. We hugged and my pussy got super wet. When I heard that hoarse, rough voice of his, my body shivered. I then realized having to sleep in a room with several other people was no longer something I had to settle for. Fuck that! I was going to chill with him in his room. I didn't care how he felt about it.

"Who you here with?" he asked out of the blue.

"Cassidy," I said softly.

Jason had heard that I was tight with Cassidy. He didn't know the whole story but he gave me a hint that he was feeling some kind of way about it. His crew even looked at me sideways like I was a groupie or something. I quickly let him know that it wasn't what he thought. I was simply styling for Cassidy and that was it. Nothing more, nothing less. Besides, Cassidy was there with a chick of his own. The last thing he was thinking about was me.

"Now, give me the key to your room," I demanded boldly putting my bid in. Jason knew what it was. He knew we needed time together.

"I'm staying with you," I said.

With his crew looking at him, Jason couldn't do anything but smile and give me what I wanted. In my heart, I loved it. It was cute to me to know that I had him like he had me. You can't change history.

"Yeah, Jadakiss," I said cockily after getting his key in my hand. "You know what it is. I got it like that."

He laughed, knowing I was right. I had a place in his heart no other woman could touch no matter how long we went without seeing each other. The shit gave me a sense of entitlement so instantly, I ordered a bell cap to take my bags to Jason's room. I wanted to get a quickie in but was disappointed that Jason didn't come to the room like I'd hoped. I thought all I had to do was shake my ass real good for him while I walked and he would follow me like a lost puppy. It didn't happen that way though. He and nearly every other rapper were there on business, not pleasure. They had meetings and commitments. Fucking would have to come later.

I was bored and as I said, disappointed. The room was silent, and silence was something I wasn't used to. I hadn't come all this way to meditate. I was used to excitement. My life was filled with noise, partying, traveling, drinking, smoking, and sex. Shit, I was addicted to getting it in. So of course, sitting in a room looking stupid and twiddling my thumbs was not an option. Fuck that. I hopped on the phone, called Cassidy's jump off and we met up to get some food.

While the two of us were hanging out eating and exploring the hotel, I ran into Fab. Of course I'd seen him in Atlanta but it seemed like overnight now his face was all over the TV and his music was all over the radio. Looking at his clothes, bling and swag, he had definitely come up. The nigga was shining like new money. He was also surrounded by an entourage. Most of them were from Brooklyn. I recognized a few from my hood.

When Fab saw me, he gave me a look that I recognized. It was pretty much the look he used to give me when he was broke. It was sort of innocent. As if he liked me but didn't want to admit it or was afraid to show it. I still didn't know what that was all about. He quickly switched it up though and began to play the Fab role he'd invented to sell records. He had an image to protect.

After hugging, Cassidy's girl and I hung out with Fab and his crew. Since most of us were from the same hood, it was pretty much like a festive gathering of friends. We drank and laughed. Finally, Fab had to go. I knew I'd see him again soon though.

As the day passed, there was one event after another, one party after another. But through it all, I never saw Jason. I had no idea where he was. That kind of pissed me off because I did want some of his attention. Cassidy's schedule was tight also. He had no free time for his girl. The event really was all about business. Bored, I finally retreated back to Jason's room alone again. As I sat there flicking through television channels, I couldn't take it. I needed to do something. I'd heard earlier that Snoop was throwing a major party that night so I decided to go check it out. I had an agenda also. Shit, since I had no man, I knew the party would be a chance for me to at least find a sponsor.

Snoop's shit was off the chain. The music was loud, there was free liquor, free food and tons of potential sponsors. Among them were members of BMF. As usual, they were doing it big. I just smiled but never hung out with them. The spot was filled with Hip Hop celebrities. Snoop, Kanye West, Keisha Cole, Trick Daddy, Trina and so many others. Immediately, seeing this as more than just an opportunity to pick up a new sponsor, I realized it was a chance to make some business moves. I got my hustle on. I'd learned a lot from Dame. This was one. I'd remembered how relentless he was when promoting Roc-A-Fella. In a room like this, he would definitely be promoting so I took a page from his playbook. I started mingling and passing out my business cards, hoping to get a few styling jobs for later.

I finally left the party. Although a lot of people were there, there was still no sign of Jason. He hadn't even breezed through for even a second. The shit had me kind of down. Damn, he wasn't even my man but he had me open like that. I found myself sitting at the makeshift bus stop where the hotel guests waited for the golf carts to take them back to the villas. That was one of those types of moments I used to hate. Back then, having time to think always irked me. I guess that's why I was always making poor decisions. I was too impulsive.

Anyway, at that moment my mind was on Jason when someone came up and sat down next to me. At first, I didn't bother to look and see who it was. When I finally did, I recognized him immediately. He'd disrespected me in New York a couple of months back for no damn reason. I didn't know whether to roll my eyes at him, say what I really felt or use my hands. I'd been around Swizz a lot and had gotten a little bit more cocky and inconsiderate like him. Somehow, he broke the ice. And within the first two minutes of our conversation, the rapper known as The Game apologized to me for the way he treated me at The W Hotel- Times Square a few months prior.

I had originally met Game while Webb and I were hanging out in Queens. Webb knew him and took me with him that night to pick Game up from the studio. Afterward, we made small talk, nothing serious. At that time, Game hadn't blown up yet. He was a nobody, but he had a sense of humor that made me laugh so I enjoyed hanging with him. That was it and that was all. There was no type of attraction. The three of us laughed and chopped it up with no problem.

Before long, we all ended up back at the W Hotel. While there, we smoked good weed and drank a few bottles of Moet. I didn't see any problem with being in a hotel room with two guys because Webb and I were cool. We went way back so I knew I could trust him.

Webb got a phone call. When he hung up, he said he had to make a run and that he would be right back. Being left alone with Game didn't bother me. Game seemed cool and we were having some deep talks, especially about some of the rappers with whom he was having problems. He named names but I'll keep those names quiet ...for now. Anyway, everything was all good. But out of nowhere, he tried to get the panties. The way he did it didn't sit well with me at all. He started grabbing and feeling on me, with me yanking away. I felt totally disrespected and I let him know it wasn't going down like that. "I'm not with all of this," I told him. He immediately got pissed. I guess he'd felt that because he was a rapper, although unknown at the time, every woman was just supposed to jump up out their drawers for him. Also maybe because I was in a hotel room with him. Whatever he thought, when I turned him down it made him mad.

"You can leave then," he yelled showing no remorse. Gladly, I grabbed my shit and hit the door. I put the shit behind me and never even said anything to Webb about what had happened.

By the time the golf cart finally pulled up, Game had apologized for trying to rough me up that night. Looking him in the eyes, I could see his words were genuine. If you want to know when someone's lying, just look him in the eyes. The eyes never lie. He asked me to go back to his villa with him while guaranteeing he wasn't going to try anything. He was just as bored as I was and just needed somebody to kick it with. I should've said 'hell no'. I know that. I don't know why I agreed. Fuck, I don't know why I did a lot of the things I did in my life. I just did them. I do know, though, he said he had plenty of weed. And Lord knows I'm a damn crack head for weed.

We ended up chilling in his room and talking. As we spoke, he kept saying I was ghetto. He said that I was so ghetto he couldn't understand chicks like me. That was strange. He was supposed to be from Compton. How much more hood was anything than that? But yet he didn't act like it. Honestly, he was kind of corny. He wasn't what I was used to. Maybe because he was from California, clear across the country from me.

Anyway, we drank and smoked as time passed by with him cracking silly jokes. Before I knew it, I was wasted. Not totally wasted but I was getting there. The combination of good weed and wine had done a number on me. But through it all, my mind kept wondering about Jason. I wondered if he'd made it back to the room yet.

Eventually, the sun began to come up. Game surprised

me by asking me to get in his Jacuzzi with him. I wasn't feeling that. Even though my mind was full of weed I wanted to check to see if Jason was back at the room. I told Game I had to run back to my room and get a bathing suit. I swear on everything I love that my intentions were to get out of there and never come back. Jason was who I wanted to be with so I left and headed back to Jason's room looking forward to being in his arms. But when I got there, the room was just the way I'd left it.

Jason wasn't there and hadn't been there. I got mad. What kind of business could he be handling that would keep him gone all night? Immediately, I jumped to conclusions and figured he was with another bitch, although he'd never played me like that before. Out of spite, I returned to Game's room. When Game opened the door he was dripping wet and dressed in just his boxers. His body was tight, and he was tatted up all over. He shut the door and I followed him out to the Jacuzzi. Game hopped in and with no shame, pulled me in with him. The moment seemed weird. There weren't many times where I was with someone who just chilled in a situation like that. Eventually we just talked, with the jets shooting out pressure all around us; my body leaned back against his chest. They say everything happens for a reason...enough said.

I have nothing but the deepest respect for The Game.

14 Hustlin'—Grindin'

The Puerto Rico trip ended well, with me finally getting with Jason before I left. Although the sex had improved the relationship was dwindling—fast, and I knew it. I just wanted us to at least maintain our friendship. After all he'd known me longer than any other man I still kept in touch with. Jason continued to make my goal difficult. He kept doing shit to irritate me, trying to make me explode.

I saw him months later in Jacksonville at the Superbowl festivities. It was the perfect place to attend several parties back to back. My homegirl and I showed up at the club where Jada would perform. We texted his homeboy who got us into the club where we all partied and had a good time. Drinks were flowing but the mood was crazy. Out of the blue, Jason started acting funny again, like he didn't know me. That was it. I blasted off on him, repeating all the same shit we'd been going through lately. "You letting this success shit go to your head," I said loudly. "Remember, I knew you when you had nothing."

"I'm just acting the way you acting," he replied.

Yet even though I had grown tired of his bullshit over the last few years I spent the next two nights with him in

Jacksonville where I put it on him, reminding him of what he'd been missing. His sex was the best he'd given me in a while. Not because I was in love with him, but because I had love for him and how he'd been a part of my life for so long.

Not long after the Superbowl, Webb got ahold of me and asked if I wanted to do some work with him. Him and Cheo were doing well as Fab's managers, which blew my mind because they'd all come a long way. Never in a million years did I expect them to one day manage one of the hottest rappers in the industry. They'd once been street dudes grinding their way to the top. They'd definitely gotten focused; left the knuckle head shit alone and were now about legitimate business. I was so proud.

I started working for them within weeks. It was nothing major. I would do simple tasks like scheduling, typing up contracts, handling riders and tasks with the accountant. It didn't pay much but it was a side hustle while making my styling career happen. Also, it helped beef up my resume.

Although the pay was weak, I enjoyed working for Cheo and Webb and went above and beyond with my duties. They always treated me with respect and always kept our relationship professional. That made me feel comfortable and appreciated so I never wanted to disappoint. I stayed just as professional as they did and kept a positive attitude even during days when life had me down. Everyone felt comfortable around me and liked the real, wild and crazy Winter. It was because of those things that they eventually recommended me to Fab when an assistant position came open.

When Fab called me in June 2005, on top of being excited, I was flattered. It meant a lot to me to know Cheo and Webb had thought enough about me to look out for me like that. I appreciated it. About business though, before accepting, I asked him the traditional questions: What would I be doing? Days off? etc, etc. Most people thought he was still signed to Atlantic Records but I knew that contract was over and Fab was searching for a new record label so I asked the most important question....What does the job pay? Now keep in mind, I'd been around enough rappers to know that most of them were broke in reality. They didn't have even half the materialistic things or money they rapped about having. Usually, the ones who bragged the most were the brokest. And if you know Fab's music, you know he's about as bragadocious as they come so I was expecting the pay to be cheap but not as cheap as what actually came out of his mouth.

"Three hundred dollars a week," he said with no shame.

Of course, that was chicken feed. I knew people making more than that flipping burgers at McDonalds or pushing a broom in some high school somewhere. Not that those jobs aren't considered a hard day's work, I just thought working for a rapper of his caliber would pay so much more. The number was insulting but I knew Fab was on the rise. His name was getting hotter and hotter. So I figured if I accepted the pay, proved my loyalty and went hard at my job, it would eventually pay off. More money would come. Besides, I was still getting money from Jason whenever I needed it.

Jason's pockets weren't as deep as anyone would expect but he had a generous and kind heart. If I needed something, no matter what, I could go to him. So combining the little bit of money he gave me with the money I was making from my styling jobs and now would be receiving from Fab would keep my pockets straight. And if crunch time arrived, it would be nothing to hit the club, bait me in a boss, and play around in his pockets as usual. Not bragging. It is what it is. I'm like a cat, always landing on my feet.

So, my life with Fab began.

The very first thing I noticed was that Fab no longer resembled that boy he'd been back in that hole in the wall apartment just before his first album dropped. That dude was long gone. Now he was cockier, more experienced and even a little stuck up. Also, the feelings he had for me that were so obvious back then were now not so obvious now. At times, they seemed non-existent. The industry had hardened his heart. That was cool. I wasn't looking for a relationship with him. The goal was to build my resume in the music industry.

My duties started off with general stuff, mainly administrative, like booking hotel rooms and flights. I took care of things in his personal life like making sure he made it to places on time, returned important phone calls; showed up for interviews, promo events, photo sessions, and studio time. In the beginning, it was a tedious process that took a lot of patience because Fab was notorious for being late to anything and everything. It took a lot of pushing. And obviously for what he was paying, it wasn't worth it but I stuck with it.

In no time, his reputation for being late changed and people in his circle applauded me, knowing I was the reason. It got to the point where they were bragging about the way I carried things out.

During that time, Fab also watched me very closely. He'd been in the industry long enough to have come across plenty of people who hadn't had his best interests in mind. He'd met plenty of snakes who'd smiled in his face then stabbed him in the back when he wasn't looking. So I could understand his apprehension. These days, I don't trust too many people my damn self. I knew our relationship had gotten more into the trust zone the first time he wanted me to spend the night at the house with him and his boys. It was also the night when I began keeping a journal. I figured my new life with him would take me places and have me seeing things most would never experience.

Journal Entry

I hope stayin the night doesn't become frequent. These bunk beds are uncomfortable. I thought we'd be in

*nice fancy hotels or a big ole mansion but I guess every-
thing ain't what it seems. Rah is sleeping up top and I
hope he doesn't try anything. I hope I don't have to make
breakfast in the a.m. I didn't sign up for that. I need to find
a spot closer to Jersey because I can't sleep like this
again. He needs to pay me more for the overnight work. I
hate that I'm sleeping in my clothes I've been in all day...
this is gross. I'm getting up before everyone wakes up and
I'm going straight to Brooklyn.*

Our work load soon escalated. I spent a lot of time
dealing with Fab's schedule. I also eventually had to help
him with more personal situations. Thank God, I didn't have
to deal with his phones. Fab had two phones. One for his career and family. The other phone was his pop off phone for
the countless chicken heads, groupies, boppers, hoes, sluts or
whatever else you want to call them that he had scattered
across the country. There was never a shortage. He had
plenty of them so the pop off phone stayed ringing off the
hook no matter what time of day or night. The craziest part
about his phone was how he had the girls' names listed by
the abbreviated city where they were from.

A player at work.

Fab never really brought girls to the house. He preferred to take them to a hotel room, which I would usually
book. Once there, he'd bang 'em out, send them on their way
and come back like nothing ever happened. That was the first
time I really paid attention to how men viewed women and
how stupid women could be. I mean, some of them seriously
thought they had a chance at being special, Fab's one and
only. And they were willing to demean themselves and com-
promise their self-respect to achieve it, not realizing or car-
ing that he was bragging to his boys about how he'd just
smutted them out. Of course, I wondered if that was how
certain dudes in my life spoke about me when I wasn't
around. I'm now positive it was.

Anyway, as time passed, more and more tasks got added to my workload. I was now taking his jewelry to the jeweler, going with him to the grocery store and making sure everyone was at his beck and call. Basically, the work increased but the pay stayed the same. I didn't trip though. In all honesty, I liked my job and my self-esteem rose. It was mainly because of the positive changes in Fab's personal and business life due to my persistence. It felt good to know that I was having a hand in it. I mean, people around him were complimenting me on the changes they were seeing in Fab. The changes were just *that* obvious. Fab noticed them, too. I know he did. But for some reason, he rarely complimented me. Shit, the nigga would find it difficult to even say thank you. But that's just the way he was, I learned.

Despite us getting to know each other, Fab rarely showed emotions and still, we hadn't become friends. He was the boss and me - the worker. He always kept his cards close to his chest. We were alike in that way. It was the best way to keep outsiders off balance so I understood him, especially in this business. That's just the way you have to be or you'll get ran over. People will use your emotions against you.

Realizing I was pretty much a part of his life, Fab finally gave me a bin in his garage with the others who stayed at his house regularly. There were always countless guys hanging around. Everyone there had a bin with their name on it full of clothes and now mine was the newest addition. It was weird but I got used to it because I realized him giving it to me meant he was beginning to trust me more. Soon, he trusted me so much that I was staying at my place in Brooklyn less and less.

My day to day responsibilities kept growing and more time was needed with him. It was now to the point where I was even handling club outings, serving almost like his security even though he already had qualified security. Maybe it was paranoia but he wanted my eyes on him along with the eyes of his security whenever he hit the club. I understood though. With the amount of expensive jewelry he always wore, it was needed. I'm not saying he's a pussy but shit, Fab is only a buck forty-five soaking wet. You do the math. One slap or punch, and he'd probably fold like lawn furniture. The shit would be all over YouTube. Obviously, no one wanted that. Besides, in my heart he'd become family.

I found myself becoming overprotective of Fab. Looking out for him became much more than just a job; it became a way of life. I'd grown so used to it that I just couldn't help it. People who knew us would always ask me why I was like that with him. They immediately jumped to the conclusion that I was fucking him. No matter how much I denied it, they thought what they wanted. That was their business. For me, Fab was paying me to do a job, one I took seriously.

The only thing I hated was that Fab never really showed any appreciation. I mean, here I was with him around the clock doing more than an assistant should be doing and he would rarely thank me. But once again I just chalked that up to how difficult it was for him to show his emotions. I knew deep down he cared. He just didn't know how to show it.

When you're as close to someone as I was to Fab, even in an employee/boss relationship, you can find yourself worrying about them at times. It's just a reflex. One of the things that worried me about Fab was his spending habits. At times he'd spend ten to thirty stacks in the club like it was nothing. He was so careless with money I would have to go behind him and make sure he wasn't overcharged on his credit cards. The last thing I wanted to see was him get taken advantage of or hurt. I had no idea though that I would eventually be put in a position where my life would be jeopardized too.

The pace of our lives soon escalated all too quick. I realized I'd been working for Fab for a couple of months. He'd been spoiled rotten. I was so caught up in my duties that I didn't have time for my own life. I was just barely going back to my place in Park Slope, Brooklyn where I'd been living for about six months. My styling jobs became non-existent. My life now revolved around Fab and his career. The craziest thing about it is, after all I was doing and after all the positive changes I'd brought to his life and career, he still didn't want to pay me more than three hundred dollars a week. The nigga could spend money tricking, splurge thousands at the club, spend money on hotel rooms and shopping sprees but he couldn't pay me more than three hundred dollars a week. What type of shit was that?

But for what the job lacked in pay, it more than made up for in perks. I kept the change for everything: gas, grocery store runs, the cleaners. You name it, I kept it and he knew it. I drove all five of his whips which included a Bentley, Range Rover and a Benz. When he ate good, which was pretty much every day, I ate good. When he shopped, he always bought something nice and expensive for me too. He was generous in those ways so I didn't bug him about a raise yet. Still though, despite how generous he could be, he always seemed to have a coldness about him like he didn't truly appreciate my sacrifices. Soon, I found out where that coldness came from after making several runs back and forth to the Brevoort Projects to drop off money to his mother.

Ms. Cain, Fab's mother had a very cold and mean personality, rarely offering up a smile. I'm not going to bite my tongue about it. She never made you feel warm or appreciated. She was angry at the world. She didn't even seem to show any appreciation for the things Fab did for her. It was now obvious why Fab behaved the way he did. He'd gotten it honest. His mother kept her emotions concealed and it rubbed off on him. I began to wonder if she ever told him she loved him or that she was proud of his accomplishments.

After witnessing a few of their interactions, I seriously doubt it. It was also obvious that he didn't have much growing up. That's why he always over compensated when he spent money. He wasn't used to the money. He'd never had it before.

After experiencing his mother's coldness, I saw Fab in a totally different light. I mean, I had already respected him. Now, though, I saw him as much more of a human being than a rapper, a superstar or even an employer. I realized he had problems and inner demons just like everyone else. The money, cars and fame didn't make him immune to it. It simply confirmed what others have said: rappers are real people. I became thankful that he allowed me to become a part of his inner circle. It really meant something to me because I now understood why it was so hard for him to open up to people. I began to see him as a comrade; one with whom we'd tackle the world together.

That was where our official bond began.

.

15   Wide Open

August 2005. Every hotel in South Beach was booked solid. After parties were scheduled for nearly every club and event center. Limo and car services were busier than any other time that entire year. Cameras and flashing lights were everywhere. Celebrity sightings had been reported all over the city all day long. All eyes all over the world were on Miami.

The VMAs were in town.

I'd begun to fall in love with Miami around this time. It had an atmosphere like no other city I'd been to and I'd been to a lot of them. Usually when in Miami, my eyes would be peeled for some sexy man who'd become my meal ticket, flying me all over the world. But that night I wasn't afforded that luxury. I was there on business. There would be no pleasure, just work. Fab had been grinding for days leading up to the awards show and that night was no different. Even my desire to party had subsided. Whenever free time came about, I preferred to rest rather than party. The rest never really lasted too long because it seemed like as soon as I closed my eyes, my phone would ring and I'd have to handle another matter for Fab.

The day of The VMAs, Fab called me and told me to pick up a female friend of his from the airport. She was coming in from Virginia. When he told me her name was Emily, I remembered her from the trip we'd recently taken to St. Thomas and St. Kitts. Fab and I had gone there for some Caribbean festival and Emily was the flavor of the week that had been flown in. At that time I figured he must've really liked her. My strict orders were to pick her up and book her in a hotel away from ours. She wouldn't be going to the VMAs with him. I was irritated and he probably heard it in my voice. He hadn't invited me to the VMAs either. Instead, he wanted me to chauffer around another one of his damn women. The thought pissed me off but I didn't say anything. Of course, he wasn't obligated to take me to the VMAs. I wasn't his woman but damn. After busting my ass for him, he could've at least offered.

Nonetheless, I did what he asked. I scooped Emily up from the airport and got her situated. Since neither of us received an invite to the VMAs and had nothing else planned, we decided to get some wine, order some room service and chill. Why not make the best out of a boring situation? Emily turned out to be mad cool. We sat and talked about damn near anything and everything. It was through that conversation that I discovered she had a past with Fat Joe, Dwyane Wade and a few other well-known celebrities. The fact that she opened up about her personal business and had no regrets about her past made me take a liking to her. We laughed and chopped it up like old friends, enjoying each other's company.

Since she'd messed with several different celebrities, we had something in common. I could understand her, which made me like her even more. She had swag and a personality a lot different from the other women I'd seen with Fab. Most were bimbos and airheads. Emily was different. She seemed to have her shit together. I could see why Fab was interested in her.

At the time, although Emily seemed cool, I thought Fab would have his fun and send her back home like he did the rest of his girls. He was notorious for that. I'd seen so many come and go that I really didn't think she stood a chance, despite the fact that I saw something special in her. I turned out to be wrong though. Right after the VMAs, Fab did something shocking. He moved her into the hotel with us. The shit was unbelievable.

Although he still had his pop off phone, Fab was definitely feeling her. For the next two weeks while in Miami he had her with him every step of the way. Still, although I knew he was feeling Emily because he'd moved her into the hotel with us, Fab was Fab it was only a matter of time before his true colors showed. I don't know what it was like behind the closed doors of their hotel room. But when around me and everyone else, Fab gave her that intimate treatment a man is supposed to show his woman. That was rare since he rarely showed emotions. But as I said, none of his other chicks ever had the opportunity to chill with him for weeks straight so I guess that should've told me something about where their relationship was headed.

Anyway, it didn't take long for Emily's baby daddy to get wind of what was going on in Miami. From Virginia, he began ringing her cell phone off the hook, wanting to know what was going on and when she was coming home. She let us know that he was cursing her out, "Telling her to bring her ass home." He must've been seriously pissed. I don't know if it was out of jealousy or something genuine. All I know is he wasn't feeling the fact that she'd been gone so long.

Emily had left her daughter with a friend of hers while she chilled with Fab in Miami. Her baby daddy was super furious about that. She told me that he was screaming on her, saying, "You in Miami following behind that rapper." She told me he started calling her an unfit mother and threatening to get custody. I felt bad for Emily. Even though I'd only known her for a short period of time, there was no way anyone would be able to convince me she was unfit. I could clearly see how good a person she was. She loved her daughter more than life itself. She was just getting away to let her hair down for a moment. Every mother needs that now and then. She knew her daughter was in good hands. If she weren't, trust me; Emily wouldn't have left her.

Her daughter's father was probably pissed because Emily was fuckin' with someone who could give her and their daughter something much more than he could. Fab felt sorry for Emily's situation so in a matter of weeks he invited her to go back to Jersey with us when he was finished with his Miami business. She accepted and rolled with us back to Jersey. His place only had three bedrooms so I was curious as to how that would work out and how long. But above all, I wondered if she would get a bin with her name on it too. The rest of us had to earn ours.

A week after we got back to Jersey Emily left to go back to Virginia. At first, I thought it was for good until I realized Fab's Range Rover was gone. Shortly after, Emily showed back up with her daughter. Not only did she come back with her daughter, she came back with her dog, Chloe, too…and all her personal belongings. My mouth dropped.

Emily's been sharing Fab's bed ever since. I guess my question was answered. She earned her spot. Despite Fab's lack of showing emotion, things were working out surprisingly. But as I had already discovered and Emily had already learned through experience, being with a celebrity is a difficult task. There's lots of competition. Because of that, things didn't stay too rosy in paradise for long. Emily was a trooper though. She put up with more than I think I would've.

After Emily moved in, I continued to stay at the house often. I was there with two other guys that I shared a room with. It wasn't lavish but I made do. I constantly had a job to do so I never really paid attention to the living conditions. As long as they respected me and my space, I respected theirs and everything was all good.

Shortly thereafter we were all back on the road again. We went back to Miami on business to record Fab's album. Fab left Emily behind though. The reason was obvious. Once in Miami, he was back to his womanizing. It was like that from that point forward. I had to admit, I felt bad for Emily. The two of us were turning into good friends. I liked her and felt she deserved better. But Fab was my boss. I had to stay loyal to him. Surprisingly, even though Emily and I were becoming friends, she never asked me anything about Fab's infidelities, or anything that would've jeopardized my job. I wouldn't have told her anyway but I was still surprised. Curiosity would've had me asking all types of questions. Emily was different, just plain classy. Plus, I'm pretty sure she knew what was going on anyway. She'd been around enough rappers to know they rarely stayed faithful. She just chose not to make a big deal out of it. For whatever her reasons were, she just played her position because no matter how many females he was fucking, Emily was the one he loved. I respected her for that.

Things began to take off for Fab even more around this time. His name had grown larger and more notable. As he became more popular my responsibilities increased. Work became more tedious and time consuming but I handled it. I found myself in October of 2005 in New York at another video shoot. Surprisingly, it was for Blue. Fab was being featured in the video. More importantly, I discovered someone else whom I was already diggin' and would soon grow almost infatuated with. He was featured also. I won't say his name and will just call him "Big Money," my corporate thug.

Filming of the video, "The Streets on Lock" took place at the perfect time. But I didn't look too hot with my scarf on my head and shades over my eyes. Baby Blue was pretty much stalking me though, despite my appearance. The two of us were still lightweight fooling around since Atlanta. For me, it wasn't serious. I'd grown bored with him but he caught feelings and still felt like it was serious. I led him on, I'll admit. I had to. The nigga had money and I never knew when I might come across a moment when I would need some.

While I was pretending with Baby Blue, my eyes were on Big Money. I mean, I was peeping his every move. I had a huge crush on him despite only seeing him on a flyer in Rucker Park. Since Smiley, I wasn't in too much of a hurry to fall in love but Big Money had me thinking about it. He could get it, fa real. The only problem was he didn't know I existed. He wasn't paying the slightest bit of attention to me. He'd seen me handling a few tasks for Fab but that was it.

After doing a club scene, the video was finally over and everyone decided to go to a bar that night. While there, I noticed Big Money sitting in a secluded part of the bar by himself. He was wearing dark glasses, which was weird because the club was mad dark. He had security but it was thin. He hadn't blown up yet, at least not across the country. He was large across the south. But as far as the rest of the world, he was a new artist with one song out at the time. He finally noticed me and appeared to be signaling me to come to his table. Like an airhead I looked around, thinking he had to be talking to someone else. The man I had such a huge crush on *couldn't* be telling *me* to come to his table. Come to find out, he was. I got up and headed over to him. Thinking there had to be a catch, I asked, "What you need? Something for Fab?"

"Nah", he said. "I want *you*."

Breathlessly, I had to keep my composure. His voice had me spellbound. It was the same voice I'd heard on the radio in ATL when I was in the car with Baby Blue. Even though I realized it the first time I heard him speak…just being up close and personal with him did something to my insides. Instead of showing him I was into him, I simply asked, "Why are you wearing those shades? It's dark in here."

"I don't like people looking in my eyes."

We talked for a while and he eventually asked me to come back to his hotel room. I declined though, knowing Fab would be furious if I did. He hated me dating guys in the business. Besides, I had to play hard to get. The two of us agreed to meet up the next day though. He took me out and we ended up back at his hotel that night. That's when I got to see his eyes for the first time. More importantly, I got to see the *real* him, the one who wasn't in the media or on stage. It was interesting and a turn on. During that night, he tried to get some ass. As bad as I wanted to give it to him, I had to turn him down. There were two reasons. One: I didn't want to hear Fab's mouth. He and Fab were close and I didn't want to put my job on the line. Two: I was really feeling Big Money. I wanted his respect. I wanted to be more than just a booty call or one night stand. I wanted his heart. It was weird how from the moment I heard his voice on the radio for the first time in Atlanta to the time I saw his face on a flyer, there had been this strong desire for him. It's unexplain-able...just a deep connection that I felt. Real talk: I wanted him to eventually become my husband.

Instead of sexin', we spent the entire night talking. He seemed to be curious about me and my personal life so I told him a whole lot. I shared my dreams. He, on the other hand, didn't share too much. I guess he was feeling me out. That was understandable. I didn't mind. Plus, I'd heard some-where that he preferred to keep his personal life just that...personal. When he did open up to me, it was mainly about his plans for the future, his career and the industry. He was cocky. Some would say a little too cocky. I loved it though. Confidence turned me on and was the easiest way to get at me. Especially when the man who possesses the talent is determined to make things happen.

Big Money kept me smiling that night. He kept me in awe. I loved that about him. That night turned out to mean more to me than any orgasm could. The next night though, I needed more than just his words. I needed more than just his look or touch. I couldn't hold back.

I needed him inside of me.

Our third night went a little something like this....In the king-sized bed of his suite, we tackled one another onto the bed....The moment he entered me I felt like we were consummating something real. I had craved this man for so long. But to my disappointment he was small....real small...yet for the first time in my life I was okay with that. I wanted more than just his sex. Big Money gave me passion. He was the one who could put a smile on my face the moment I heard his voice or saw his face. At the time, I figured we'd get some sex toys later or something to help him in the size department. That's when it dawned on me, from the moment I'd heard his voice I knew we were soul mates.

From that point on I would've been willing to break a leg just to get with him whenever time permitted. For months I craved to be with him, almost thirsty, which was so different from the way I felt about guys before.

One day while at Fab's house, I sent Big Money a picture via email. I thought he would just comment on the picture. Instead, he responded:

Come to Miami.

My heart pounded as I wondered how I was going to make it all work. Fab was out of town but due to come back the following day. I asked Emily if she thought I should go. She gave me the go ahead. Next thing I knew, Big Money had purchased the ticket and I flew out.

He was in Miami to work on his second album so I knew his time would be split between me and the studio.

Still, I loved Miami and I now loved "Big Money."
The word 'love' now had me feeling crazy; I still couldn't believe he had me feeling that way. I arrived in town and we ended up at the Shore Club. Our two day rendezvous was filled with lots of studio time and moments where Big Money would have me listening to his new songs that hadn't been released yet. I truly enjoyed those moments with him. It gave me a chance to see how really determined he was with his career. We even ended up spending a night at the Hit Factory and I realized that he didn't just talk to me about his goals and dreams, he really was ambitious.

Journal Entry

Is this fool serious? We have to listen to his song while we're having sex. I can't. This is crazy. He came off a lil cocky but I didn't think he was feeling himself this bad. At least the songs not too bad. Now everytime I hear this song I have to think about him and his lil penis. I like him though so we're gonna stick it out. Hopefully later down the line we can switch up the playlist when he puts out more music. Maybe something with one of my favorite R&B singers so I can sing along while we fuck.

Our sex life still needed work. I found out the hard way that Big Money was a selfish lover. He always wanted to get his…and that was it. No other way to put it. He was also demanding. When he wanted it…he wanted it. Still, none of that mattered. We'd gotten much closer and were taking it further and further every day. Shit, I was in love. I mean the real thing. I was head over heels for him just like I had been with Smiley so many years before. I had finally found someone I could give my heart. I had finally found someone who I felt understood me and would take care of my mind and body.
Those rare moments during which we lay in each

other's arms and passed blunts or when he'd ask my opinion about his music were dear to me. I was happy that his career had taken off. All the plans he'd discussed with me were becoming reality. The Hip Hop industry was all over him, especially the streets and specifically trap niggas. To them, he was like the next coming of Tupac. They felt no rapper could represent their pain and struggle like Big Money. His lyrics were just that realistic and his character was just that authentic. He'd really lived it. Little did I know, though, our time together would get interrupted.

Fab called spazzing out on me. He was livid. Basically he felt like I was running behind a rapper and unable to do my job. "I do my job," I roared back knowing I'd given him my all.

"And why the fuck did you go to Miami, Winter? You work for me! I need you to be available!"

That was that controlling shit I hated so much. As long as I did my job, what was the problem? It seemed like me working for him and having a relationship wasn't going to work.

Bullshit!

My 2nd Christmas – Spoiled by my mom

Yep… all those gifts for me

Spoiled brat on Easter

Me at seven years old

Photo shoot in the high school cafeteria (cutting class)

High school graduation – Nikeya, Mijiza, LaVaonne & me

Me and Spliff in Miami

Me and Busta at
Spliff & Ayanna's wedding

Me and my mom at my
21st birthday party

Me and Fab in Atlanta

Jadakiss chillin' on the bus

Me and Cassidy backstage at BET

Me and Game in Puerto Rico

Me and Ja Rule at Latin Quarters

16   That Life

Fab's career continued to blow up. 2006 came around far too quickly but it ended up being one of the most memorable years of my life. I ended up traveling to places I least expected. Some places not so fabulous like when we went to Poland and I got left behind because Fab took the last seat on the flight.

Journal Entry

This asshole left me and Tykie in Poland at this airport. Some fucking racist ass country and I'm sure he's on the plane checking MySpace and not even givin' a fuck about if we're getting home. Oh well I shouldn't expect anything else from Fab and his selfish ass. I guess I'll have to make the best of the situation. No one speaks English-FUCK. Tykie thinks this shit is funny. I'm gonna kick his ass before we leave this stupid ass country. This seat that I turned into a bed is so uncomfortable and this burger that Tykie brought back from the airport restaurant is gross. This can't be beef. I'll starve and die in Poland and Fab will be on MySpace during my funeral.

Then there were more glamorous times like when we took a private jet to Canada for a performance. Fab's career had skyrocketed. He was in demand everywhere so the Canada trip was a promo event to capitalize on it. It was work as usual for me, no fun, although I loved the fact that we got to ride on a private jet. Something about that experience excited me, knowing that I would write about it in my journal that night. I loved the fact that we didn't have to deal with long lines or getting our bags checked. We just drove right up to the plane, hopped out the car, climbed on and went about our business. It was on the jet that Fab told me he'd talked to Jay-Z and was in negotiations with Def Jam.

The next few months were crazy busy. There were constant radio and print interviews along with all sorts of invites and bookings to perform. I was excited for Fab's career but also excited for myself. He had trained me to become an amazing assistant. I no longer saw being an assistant as work or a job. I saw it as a craft. I saw it as something only few have the patience and people skills to do. And I had mastered it. With Fab, I'd visited wonderful places, met countless important people, made numerous connections, built a reputation and knew I was poised to eventually do bigger and better things. But nothing meant more than knowing that I had played a huge part in Fab's turnaround. Yes, his talent got him to where he now was. But my patience and nurturing skills helped. There was also another achievement that had a lot of importance to me…

My relationship with Big Money.

Since we'd been doing our thing, I'd had millions of chances to get with other cats. I was always being approached. Men were always promising and offering me things. Damn near not a day passed by without someone showing interest in me. But I always turned them down. I had gotten serious about Big Money. As close as we were becoming, it was looking like we were really going to be something special. It looked like he was the man I'd been waiting for all my life, and I was ready to slow down and be his wife. He had me just that fuckin' gone. But instead, I was handed disappointment and bullshit.

I ended up seeing him at the Superbowl festivities in Detroit of that same year. Thinking we were all good, I was ready to schedule my sneak away from Fab, when my eyes spotted Big Money in the club with a chick. At first I couldn't confirm if they were together. The sight sent bile rising up in my gut. I was caught off guard like a deer in headlights. It wasn't clear to me how best to handle the situation. Of course I wanted to kick his ass, but I was working as Fab's assistant and had to hold my composure. My heart told me he was with her. I'd seen rappers show up with new chicks too many times before. I don't know why I felt he would be different. When they blow up and everyone begins to pay attention to them, they forget about the one who loves them.

Finally, I got up enough nerve to approach him. "You really here with a chick?"

First came the sigh…then the bullshit.

"You're not here with me, you're with Fab," he said bluntly.

Big Money was right and I knew Fab and others were watching. I had no choice but to fall back. Still, I couldn't shake my emotions as I walked away.

Man, talk about *hurt*? I was shattered. My heart dropped to my feet. I then realized my mother was wrong. I was born with tear ducts. Tears welled up in my eyes. My world felt like it was completely destroyed. I was also angry at myself. I couldn't believe I'd let a man, a rapper, get me open like that. I couldn't believe I had exposed myself for another let down.

Right after the Super Bowl, Big Money began calling me. He swore up and down that the chick he'd been seen

with wasn't 'bout nothin'. There was nothing going on between him and her. Around that time, rumors were flying all
over the place that he was also sleeping with some R&B
chick. He denied that also. He actually swore on his son.
How classic is that?

He blamed the rumor on a bunch of nosey people who
didn't know what they were talking about, had nothing better
to do with their time and who just wanted to get some shit
started. It was obvious he was doing me bad but I was in
love. It was plain and simple as that. I'd done the same thing
to plenty of guys and was seeing Fab do it to plenty of
women. But when you're in love with someone, you tend to
give them the benefit of the doubt. You don't want to believe
they would hurt you so you ignore shit, hoping with all your
heart it's not what it really is. And in my case, I realized I'd
been searching for what me and Smiley once had for so long
that I just didn't want to accept that it didn't exist.

Against my better judgment, I believed him. Yeah, I
know.

He ended up flying me down to Atlanta to chill with
him, with the intent on making amends. He spoiled me with
his time and affection, which seemed genuine. My feelings
grew deeper, especially after the love making. Obviously,
things are said and done in the bedroom during the heat of
the moment, things that make you love that person more than
before. Those things, combined with how he'd been treating
me since he brought me down to the ATL had me gone over
his ass once again. We seemed good; no more drama so I
headed back to my life and my job, not knowing there was
more drama ahead. This time, though, the drama wouldn't
come from my relationship with Big Money.

Memorial Day of that year rolled around. Fab was hosting a party at Club Prive` in Miami. The place was wall to wall packed. Music blaring, bottles popping and celebrities mingling. Fab and I had about twenty people of our own with us. We always rolled deep, mainly for security reasons. There was never no telling when someone would try to run on Fab and become an overnight celebrity. Among our crew was a dude named Ruggs. Ruggs was wild and liked to have fun, even though his type of fun wasn't always good for him or the people around him.

As we were all sitting at our tables in the second floor section of the club, Jim Jones and his crew walked in. Chrissy was also with him but we never made eye contact. Before long, for whatever his reasons were, Ruggs decided to go fuck with Jim. At that time, I didn't think anything of it but I wish I had because on purpose or simply because he was drunk, Ruggs knocked over a bottle Jim Jones was drinking.

All hell broke loose.

An argument started between Ruggs, Jim and Jim's crew. Seeing the argument and after having words with Ruggs, Fab went over to talk to Jim alone. He knew tempers were still flaring and the argument could go further if he didn't do something to diffuse it. For once, we weren't joined at the hip. I wasn't with him as he made his way across the club but I got word that he and Jim talked. He apologized to Jim about what had happened and told him he had no idea why Ruggs did what he did. Jim accepted Fab's apology and things were good. But not for long.

About twenty minutes later, Ruggs went back over to Jim again and started fuckin' with him, kicking over some bottles of champagne, acting wild and crazy. Both crews began yelling and making threats. Things were beginning to get physical when security finally stepped in and calmed things down. Both crews went back to their sides of the club.

Someone in Jim's crew told security and security told the club's owner. The owner had zero tolerance at that point. He didn't want a repeat of what had happened earlier and he definitely didn't want to take a chance on getting his club torn up so he told Fab and the rest of our crew we had to leave. It seemed unfair, but now I realize you've got to be careful about the people you let roll with you. Since they come from the street and have no concept of keeping things professional, they will fuck things up for you in a minute. They will put you in some crazy positions. And I was getting ready to find out just *how* crazy.

We left the club and headed to the parking lot but Fab refused to leave. He wanted to hang around and diffuse things with Jim. He didn't want Jim to think he'd sent Ruggs over to fuck with him again. Whatever Ruggs was on, that was his own business. Fab wasn't being a punk, he just didn't want beef. He just saw a bigger picture. He knew eventually everyone would see each other back in NY and things could escalate. The streets could possibly get involved and someone would get hurt or possibly killed.

As we were waiting, Miami PD took notice. Seeing a group of black men hanging out probably made them nervous. They figured we were up to no good so they watched us carefully. Jim finally came out with about eight of his homies. Chrissy was with him also. Immediately, I tried to make eye contact with her, hoping as women we could diffuse anything that might go wrong. I figured if we could have talked, she would be able to speak some sense into Jim if need be. It turned out to be too late though.

Shaq, Fab's best friend saw where things were headed and quickly stepped ahead and yelled, "Yo, Jim, Fab just wants to talk to you."

Shaq had a level head and was one who knew the beef needed to be squashed. From what I saw, Jim was making his way alone towards us. Fab and his security headed towards him. They were going to talk things out. But suddenly shots rang out. Everyone ducked and began to scatter. My heart began to pound. I didn't know where the shots were coming from, who was firing them or who was hit. I just ducked for cover and ran like everybody else. People were screaming. It was chaos. The next thing I knew, I felt a sharp pain in my arm and leg. It stung and burned like hell. I knew I was shot. At that time, I also saw Fab grab his leg. He'd been shot too. We were both trying to figure out what had just happened to us. Thank God we discovered shortly after, we'd been shot with BB guns.

That night had me shook. It also opened up my eyes that I would always be put in dangerous situations while working for Fab, possibly ending my life. It wasn't Fab who was the problem, it was the company he kept. But life as an assistant doesn't stop or even slow down. Money still had to be made, business still had to be handled and mouths had to be fed. Like nothing ever happened, Fab got back to working on his album. We'd been staying in Miami for weeks and still had at least another month to go before he was done. While in Miami I talked to Big Money whenever I could.

Months flew by but as soon as a little personal time slipped through I met up with Chrissy at Chynae's spot back in New York. Chynae had been leasing the place from Chrissy ever since she'd moved in with Jim. Chrissy and I spoke about what had happened back in Miami between Fab and Jim. Our accounts didn't match up. I'm not saying she's lying. I'm just saying they were different. From where she was standing, she possibly saw things another way.

Anyway, we didn't sweat what had happened. As long as no one got hurt or killed, it didn't seem to be worth our time. We knew the blogs, magazines and radio stations were making the beef bigger than what it really was so we left it alone. In the meantime, the two of us got to know each other a little more and began to hang out much more. That would eventually become a problem for Fab.

With everything that was going on in his career he did-n't have time to figure out why I'd started hanging out at Chrissy and Jim Jones' house more often. I never tried to ex-plain….but eventually I took over Chynae's apartment and began sub-leasing from Chrissy. Chrissy and I began spend-ing lots of time together; mostly shopping, chilling and watching TV. Fab never knew where I had moved to…I never told him. I'd learned a lot. Like Fab and Big Money- I had their same mentality….my personal business was just that…personal.

Before I knew it we were headed out of town again, this time for his European tour, which was huge. In Europe they treated him like he was Michael Jackson. The girls actu-ally cried and fainted when they saw Fab. With at least five cities on the tour the most memorable was London. We stayed in a hotel directly across the street from Buckingham Palace. I was amazed, getting a chance to see all the statues and historical surroundings near the palace. Of course I loved the fact that I had the opportunity to see the famous clock, Big Ben. Those times made my experiences with Fab all worth it.

Ray J was also on tour with us. We spoke a few times and chilled but nothing worthy of discussing. He was cute and I'd heard he was bomb in bed but we never had any dealings with each other sexually. The tour was strictly work related.

The only thing I didn't like was the weather over there. It was always bad. When I say *always*, I mean *always*. Also, despite the love Fab got, he also got a lot of hate too. He was receiving threats on a regular basis. Security had to be tight-ened, especially when he was on stage. He always wore a whole lot of jewelry on stage so security knew they had to be on point each time he performed. But while the rest of the world couldn't seem to get enough of Fab's music, I'd grown tired. Soon after we returned from the tour, Fab got caught up into some shit, landing him in jail.

I wasn't there so I can't say exactly what happened. There are now seventy sides to the story. All I know is how I felt when I rushed into that hospital and saw him hurt and handcuffed to the bed. I couldn't believe that once again he'd gotten himself into a situation because of the company he kept. When I got there I didn't see his mother or Emily and I wasn't quite sure who would come bursting into the room. I remember it being a frightening situation for me. My family felt the same way. The phone calls soon came rolling in with my mother questioning if I would still work for Fab. I told her that was my life...and what I'd signed up for.

Journal Entry

So the first fucking time I decide to not go out with this fool he gets shot. Why would these idiots think it's okay to snatch a damn chain outside the restaurant and 2 hours later not even tell Fab what they did. They getting messy and next time someone's going to get killed but I'm sure he's not going to say shit to them he's a fucking punk. That shit did scare the fuck out of me. When Chrissy walked up to me in the club to tell me I saw worry in her face something I had never seen before so I knew something was terribly wrong. Good thing Chink and Rule were at the club to calm me down before I headed out the club. And the news spread so quickly. That def felt like something out of a movie. Everything in slow motion as Chrissy and Chynae walked me out the club. I could barely breathe. I thought the worse but thank goodness it was only a bullet through the leg. But now we have to deal with these gun charges. My family gonna have a fit and there is no way in hell I can lie or hide it. I hope Al can get them off. And the fact that the rest of the crew are locked up means I'll be spending the next few days in court and at the bail bondsman office. Def not part of the job but I can't leave my boys in there. Crazy thing is I'm not afraid for my own life. Does that mean I'm loyal or a damn fool?

By the time the year ended I decided to spend Thanksgiving and Christmas at Chrissy and Jimmy's house in Jersey. I had all my girls with me too…Ebony, Chynae and Sabrina. We were just kickin' it, enjoying the holidays, but of course when Fab found out he had words for me. For a while, I didn't know if Emily was the one feeding him information on my whereabouts, but I soon found the culprits. Fab and Chynae were sleeping together behind my back so it became clear how Fab knew.

Niggas and bitches.

Always up to no good.

It was just the beginning of the drama to come.

.

17   My Not So Fabulous Life

2007 arrived with me feeling differently about being around Fab so much. He had me burnt out on his voice and his music. When his song came on the radio, I turned it off. When his video came on television, I changed the channel. Nothing personal. I was just that burnt out. Hearing his voice anywhere had me thinking there was work to do. It had even gotten to the point where when he did a collaboration with Swizz, I didn't even want to roll with him to the studio. I never wanted Fab to know I'd messed around with Swizz anyway.

It seemed like since my relationships were mostly based around people in the music industry it was becoming more difficult keeping my personal business away from Fab. Being sneaky had become a part of me and always came into play simply because I worked for him. All Star Weekend 2007 proved to be no different.

Once again the words 'passion, excitement, desire and joy' all filled my gut the moment my plane landed. That's what I'd always read love was supposed to feel like. This was it. *He* was the one. The man who'd swept me off my feet....in private of course. Still, our relationship was hush

hush to both the public and his fans, and only a select few knew of our rendezvous. So the Vegas trip was well needed. One potential problem faced us though. It was All Star weekend and both of our schedules were jam packed.

As we raced through the airport tons of onlookers gawked at Fab, me, and the rest of our entourage from afar, pointing, grinning, snapping pictures, and some scantily dressed females even tried to rush us. Clearly, my job as Fabolous' assistant didn't involve muscle, so I moved to the side to let his bodyguard do his job and fight off the groupies. Traveling with Fab and the other Def Jam heavyweights always proved to be exciting, and this trip would be no different. Before I knew it car service arrived, and I commenced to secretly dialing my man's cell number. My intent was to get Fab and the other guys checked in then flock over to Big Money's hotel room. As the phone rang that strong desire to be with him filled me again. The thought of hearing his raspy voice sent chills up and down my spine while the loud chatter around me continued.

It didn't take long for me to realize he wasn't answering, but I'd been determined my entire life. I hung up, called again, and paid attention to the fast pace of my heart beat. Again, no answer. That incident got brushed under the rug quickly, since my duties began as soon as we pulled up to the hotel. Within an hour, we were all checked in, and the entourage headed to Fab's first radio interview. Since this was some type of Def Jam takeover, I was sure Big Money would be there. He and Fab had the same sort of celebrity status by now, and my sources had previously told me they were both scheduled to do the interview.

It seemed as if the radio interview began and ended before I even realized we were all being ushered back out the door. The fact that my boo never showed up hit me like a ton of bricks. I stood for minutes with my mouth hung open. If his interview had been cancelled or postponed, where in the hell was my phone call? My insides boiled. I was pissed. What about all those words he'd spat to me over the phone or when we were getting it in back in Atlanta? I was his homie, his ride or die chick, and now I couldn't get a fucking phone call? Next thing I knew, my fingers were attacking the key pad on my phone.

It rang.

No answer.

I hung up and called again.

It rang.

And rang.

And rang.

I did the repeat thing again becoming a borderline stalker. Strangely, this time he answered. Even though steam flowed from my head, I still wanted to be in his presence and loved the sound of his confident voice. It was the same range most fans noticed when they listened to his music. I needed to get with him, fast.

"What up? Where you at?" My words quickly rolled off my tongue.

"Out," he told me.

His voice sounded so nonchalant. My first thought was to bust off on him, but my sentiment changed all too fast. I peeped to my right and left to see if anyone was listening to my call as we stepped back into the ride. The coast seemed to be clear with no one paying me any attention as the car pulled off, so I asked boldly, "Where you staying at, so I can come over?"

He paused, then hit me with, "I don't know."

Lies, I told myself. But why?

Faster than I could even blink, he man-handled me off the phone. He was a fast talker, sweet talker, and so much more when it came to women, so I knew smoke was being blown up my skirt. I took the snub like a big girl and went back to planning for Fab's appearance at a local club, which was scheduled for midnight. I wondered if Fab knew what I was trying to do since my mood had gone from sweet to sour in less than an hour. He never said much, only shot me a few looks since I took care of my job like a real woman was supposed to. I put love aside momentarily, attended the party that night, only to have my boo not show up there either. When would the lightbulb go off? Obviously, I was being played.

The next morning reality struck, an insider, one I'd like to call an informant unloaded what felt like a ton of bricks. When the words, "Your man showed up after you left," escaped his lips, I froze. Then he hit me with," *He* was with *her*."

I became over the top angry. Who was 'her?' Who was my baby with, I wondered? "Who was it?" I blasted. My source was clearly afraid of what my next reaction would be. His voice cracked. Afterwards, his throat cleared a few times. "The R&B chick that we've all heard the rumors about."

My eyes blurred. I could only see red. I knew who my informant was talking about. I was ready to fight. It was time to whip them both on contact. It took hours for my homies to calm me down. Tears flowed like the Nile, and nothing could stop my rage. Soon, nighttime fell again, and the Def Jam family had yet another event. I showed up, did my duties for Fab with a drab attitude, and attempted to settle my nerves. That's when things spiraled out of control. My multi- platinum selling dude walked in the door with the woman I suspected he was with. They were arm and arm like a real couple....like I didn't exist.

Within seconds, I wanted to charge them both. My hands shook, and my mental shifted to something similar to a mass attack. I didn't care that she was famous, or if any pictures of me going wild would be posted on the blogs. I just refused to get treated badly when he was the one stringing me along. I could've handled the truth, but not the humiliation. Clearly, I was being fucked with no vaseline. That was it...the end to our relationship as far as I was concerned. My heart may have been crushed but I held my head high, refusing to let yet another negative situation with a man ruin my job. I was able to take care of myself and used that set back as another opportunity to make myself stronger. As usual, I took a mental note of just another game that had been played.

Of course when I got the chance I wrote about his ass in my journal. At that moment I realized I was living in denial. Big Money didn't give a shit about my feelings. I knew I needed to go back to the old Winter. I did just that.

Journal Entry

So I guess it's fuckin' true. Why didn't I listen to the blogs and everybody else trying to warn me. So because my mother wasn't a fiend I guess I get the short end of the stick. Fuck him and that tough love shit he talks about. I know I'll probably take his stupid ass back but I swear I'm going to stay away as long as possible. He has to pay for this. I should fuck with one of his boys but none of them would be worth it and he would probably never fuck with me again. I'm such a sucka for this wack ass country boy. But why??? What is it about him? I'm so confused I need to see a shrink about this. This can't be healthy. Out of all of them, why him?

Of course Fab still expected me to be on point as his assistant. No rest for the weary. That spring, a twenty city promo tour, which included Atlanta, Baton Rouge, Dallas, Sacramento, and Jacksonville, Florida had been planned by the label. The entire tour was done by tour bus. It was a month and half, but loads of fun. Nearly every moment between shows was filled with partying, smoking, drinking, shopping, and eating. I enjoyed myself. The only thing I didn't enjoy was the obvious change in Fab. It was drastic. I don't know if it was personal problems, him being nervous about the upcoming album release, or him allowing his celebrity to go to his head. Whatever it was, things between us began to change for the worse and I could see the writing starting to appear on the wall.

It seemed as if my every move was being questioned. His trust in me had never been questioned before. During this time I met Ne-Yo and fell in love with the song, "You Make Me Better," all over again where he'd joined forces with Fab. It may seem crazy but I'd always thought that video was about me. The Spanish girl in the video plays security for Fab. I thought about how it related to the two of us so much. Although I was never Fab's official security I took care of him, always had his best interest at heart, and would never allow anyone to hurt him. To date, I feel like I truly made him better.

That video also sparked me to write something about Fab that should have been written earlier near my birthday. It was special but somehow intentionally overlooked.

Journal Entry

Tonight was great. My birthday dinner was perfect. I can thank Fab for that. Even in the midst of doing spring bling he planned this whole thing. Even my mother, brother and aunt were there. I hadn't spent time with them in a minute and he didn't urk me about any tedious work either. I guess he does have his good side when the hell he wants to. That dinner at Don Shulas steakhouse I'm sure set him back at least 1,000. I guess I shouldn't have expected a gift after that. But I did appreciate what he did. And I damn sure deserved it. Tomorrow we heading to Miami for more birthday fun for me. I guess I should take advantage of it shit I'll only get this treatment once a year. Kudos for loso!!!

By the time our stop in Houston rolled around, the pressure was on. Fab's album, scheduled to be released that June, had lots of buzz. Like any other artist the first week sales would mean a lot. Fab seemed extra nervous and frustrated. Somewhere in between all the work, I'd managed to call Slim Thug, a rapper from Houston who I'd had my eye on for a while. My excuse was that I'd hook him up with Fab and he could show us a good time that night in Houston.

My plan worked. Slim Thug came to the hotel and took us to the club. I orchestrated all of that. Crafty, if I must say so myself. He was just my type: fresh braids and thugged out. I had no intention of starting a relationship with him. Big Money had killed any chances of that. I just wanted a little time alone while in Houston. At the club all the homies around Fab who were on tour with us kept saying, "Winter Dog, you can't get him. That's Slim Thug."

None of them saw me as a real woman with a real life or needs. They saw me as one of the fellas. It was all fun and games until Slim Thug and me started flirting at the club. Knowing Fab would say something irked me. But I wasn't about to let that hold me back. Eventually we all went back to our hotel only I didn't go to sleep.

The knock came soon on the room's door. It was Slim Thug. That night started and ended quickly. The three hours we shared together were well worth it. The name Thug fit him perfectly since he was thugged out in the bedroom. He liked it rough and so did I. The only problem with the way that night ended was the next morning our tour bus was leaving early. By the time I made it downstairs, Cheo warned me that Fab knew. He was upset. Obviously Slim Thug had parked his pimped out Range Rover out front for all to see. I wanted Fab to stay out of my personal life the way I now stayed out of his.

18 New Money

In June of 2007, I started hanging out a lot when I could manage to get away from Fab. One night I was out at Club Lotus with my Murder Inc. family: Irv Gotti, Chris Gotti, Charlie Baltimore and Ebony. We were popping bottles as usual and having a good time when I made eye contact with some dude who was clearly undressing me with his eyes. It was that obvious. I mean, he was scouring my body from head to toe with more than just admiration. It was pure "I want you." I'd seen that look more times than I could count. Anyway, I'd seen my stalker earlier in the day down at Rucker Park where we had made eye contact there too but I had no idea who he was. All I knew was he had pretty good handles and he came down to the park to ball often. Also, each time he came, people made a huge fuss over him.

That night at the club, after staring me down for a while, he finally decided to make his way over. We were in VIP and surrounded by security so it should've been difficult for him to get anywhere near us. Instead, security parted for him like the Red Sea. Irv and Chris greeted him with daps and hugs. I knew then his status must've been important. They offered him drinks and he took a seat like he was one

157

of the family. As he conversed with Irv and Chris, his eyes always seemed to make their way to me. Finally, he made his move.

He introduced himself as Rafer Alston.

We began to talk. He had a New York accent and since I'd seen him ball at the Rucker, I figured he lived in New York. Come to find out he was born and raised in Queens but he now lived in Houston. Also, it turns out he was a street ball legend. The streets called him Skip to My Lou. I discovered that after noticing everyone calling him Skip.

He's probably going to be pissed when he reads this but I'm going to be real about it. My honesty is going to be brutal but it is what it is. Here we go. I had no physical attraction to Rafer that night. I knew he had money, otherwise he wouldn't have gotten close to Irv and Chris. But the nigga wasn't cute or handsome at all. Real talk. Also, his swag wasn't too much to brag about. I won't call it corny. It just wasn't what I was used to being in the Hip Hop scene.

Despite being unattracted to him, I spoke to him throughout the night mainly to be nice. I didn't want to hurt his feelings. We eventually exchanged numbers. I almost gave him a fake one but for some reason chose not to. Thankfully I didn't because no sooner than we parted ways, Ebony pushed up on me and put me on to who he was.

"Girl, he plays ball," Ebony said.

"I know," I told her. "I saw him at the Rucker."

"No, Winter. I mean *real* ball. That nigga is in the NBA."

No wonder I didn't give him a fake number, I immediately realized. My spidey senses had been tingling and I didn't even know it. That part of me that loved money had been the part that gave him my real number. All of a sudden, me not being attracted to him didn't bother me too much.

Rafer called me the very next day. Although his conversation bored me the previous night, I was all up on it that day. We spent a few hours getting to know each other. Then he asked me to go out with him. At first, I wasn't sure but Chrissy, Ebony and Chynae were over at the time. Each of them was all up in my ear like the good angel and the bad angel that used to sit on a person's shoulder in the old Bugs Bunny cartoons. Chrissy apparently was the good angel.

"Just give it a chance, "she said genuinely. "You need to try things out with Skip. He's a good dude. He's different from those other niggas you've been fuckin' with. You need to go out with him. Trust me: he's a real good dude."

Although she was adamant, I still had reservations until she said, "Winter, stop letting these niggas play you. It's time you start making these niggas take care of you. Here's your chance to make that happen."

Those words stuck with me. I began to think about how I'd fucked with all these different dudes and none of them had given me their all. Here was my chance to really go hard. Here was my chance to make a million dollar athlete fall in love with me and treat me like the queen I deserved. Chrissy had gone deep with her advice, and since she had experience, I decided to listen.

After deciding to go out with Skip, Chrissy snatched me into the bedroom like a rag doll. She began going through my closet looking for the perfect outfit. She put me in a black mini skirt, a cute top and a pair of Gucci sandals I'd gotten while in Miami. I felt like I was being dressed for the prom but Chrissy wanted me to look good and not dress like I was working.

Skip picked me up in his friend JR's Chrysler 300 and took me to Merchants, a steakhouse in the city. While there he finally revealed to me that he was famous and that he was an NBA player. Of course, I acted both shocked and surprised. He then told me he was currently playing for the Houston Rockets but was staying downtown for the off season.

"It's June now," I said. "How long is the off season?"

With a smile, he said, "As long as I got a reason to be here." It was obvious he wanted to get with me.

As we spoke throughout the night, I realized he had a little game. It wasn't as advanced as most people I knew but it was a little something. One thing bothered me though. I kept wondering why he was staying in a hotel. He was from New York so why didn't he have a house in the city or family he could stay with? That was strange. I'd been with enough cats to know the hotel was their jump off spot. That was where they took their One Nighters. At first I wondered if that's what Skip had planned for me. The hotel had my antennas up but I didn't question him about it. I left it alone, knowing I'd find out why soon enough.

Skip turned out to be pretty funny and down to earth. I enjoyed his company. He was intelligent, had a strong sense of humor, and was cool to be around. I know those who are reading this won't believe me. Shit, I wouldn't believe me either but at the moment I'd forgotten about his money. I really did. I began to look at him as a human being.

After that night, the two of us clicked. We were good but I didn't get a chance to truly enjoy it because Fab called with his bullshit. It was like he could smell in the air that I was having a good time and he wanted to destroy it. He now had demands on top of demands because it was only a week left before his new album would be released. He wanted me to stay at his house with him and Emily and be at his beck and call. I chose not to. I enjoyed spending time with Skip, and I enjoyed being able to come and go as I pleased without someone watching my every move.

I headed out on my second date with Skip. This time we dined at Ruth's Chris Steakhouse along with his assistant Eddie. We hadn't been out five minutes before my phone started ringing off the hook. Of course, it was Fab. At first I ignored it, hoping he would stop. He didn't. He kept calling.

Finally I answered.

"Where you at?" he asked. "You coming by the house?"

In reality, Fab wanted to monopolize my time. He wanted my life to revolve around him. At this time, I was still up on my job. I was still handling business for Fab just like I'd always done. Nothing had changed. I just wanted a night out for myself. Was that too much to ask?

I quickly discovered the phone call wasn't about business at all. As we spoke, Fab was delving into my personal business. Like he was my man or something he wanted to know what I was doing and who I was with. I tried to speak in codes, giving him one word answers. I even lied and told him I wasn't with anyone. The entire time, Skip was eyeing me, wondering what was going on. I didn't know him well enough to give him a breakdown of my and Fab's relationship and that I was pretty much an indentured servant. When I hung up, I tried to give Skip bits and pieces at first, but ended up telling him more than he needed to know about my working situation with Fab.

"I'm going to change your life," he told me. "And you need to quit your job."

After that date, Chrissy and I had another one of our sisterly sessions. During this one, she told me that she and Jim used to discuss my relationship with Big Money. She said they both felt bad for me because they knew how badly he was treating me, and that I deserved more. She was sincerely hoping I would find *more* with Skip. She was truly a Skip advocate. She felt he was really a damn good guy.

"Don't fuck it up," she would say.

By the next day, Skip had spent at least 36 of the 72 hours we'd known each other at my spot. Together we had decided he didn't need his hotel room in the city. Of course that was music to my ears because it gave me a chance to watch his ass just in case the hotel had been for One Nighters like I had suspected. It worked out pretty good. We had fun and he began telling me he never wanted to leave my side. We were playing house so much that eventually my fears eased, and I wanted to be with Skip more. But once again, Fab could smell it like a shark to blood. Fab began calling damn near every ten seconds. It was like he was turning into a stalker. He was pissing me off so bad I wanted to throw the phone across the damn room. But those annoying calls would change the course of my life.

One particular day, Fab was calling nonstop again. This time, knowing who was calling and fed up with it, Skip asked, "You get paid how much?"

I'd already told him a few days earlier so I knew he was getting ready to make an obvious point. I didn't answer.

"Exactly," he said, seeing I knew what his point was. "But yet he wants you living in his house and running around like a slave for him. You need to quit."

That was his second time saying that. And those were pretty strong words from someone I barely knew but there was truth to them. Obviously Fab wasn't paying me what I was worth and he didn't want me to have a personal life. I kept the suggestion in the back of my mind.

Anyway, a few days later Fab was supposed to appear on 106 & Park. I hadn't stayed with him the night before so I called to remind him about the event and that he was also scheduled to do Fuse TV. I told him to bring an extra outfit. He began ranting and raving about how I didn't know my job and that I wasn't handling business. None of that was true. I'd never fallen off my game. He was just angry because I wasn't living in his house anymore where he could watch me like a hawk. That truth came out when he yelled, "You haven't even stayed at the house for the past three or four nights! You don't even know the schedule."

I did know the schedule. In fact, I knew it better than he did. Not only was I still always on my job, I stayed in constant contact with Carla and Jenya, other members of the Def Jam team. Refusing to argue with him, I just simply reminded him once again to bring an extra outfit and hung up.

Later that day, I got to 106 & Park first. Fab hadn't arrived yet. Since he hadn't, Jenya, a Def Jam employee, and I decided to go to a Chinese restaurant on 57th street. We ate, chilled and passed the time. During the meal, I opened my fortune cookie. It read...

YOUR CAREER PATH WILL CHANGE.

At that moment, little did I know how true that fortune was.

We headed back to the 106 & Park studio. When we arrived, I found out Fab showed up without the extra outfit that I had reminded him *twice* to bring. All he had was the clothes on his back. He decided to pick an argument with me. He'd discovered, just like I had told him, that he was also scheduled to do Fuse TV. He went off, saying everything was my fault and that if I'd stayed at his house, none of this would have happened. He then told me I would have to go back to his house in Jersey to get him an outfit. I asked why no one else could bring him an outfit but it fell on deaf ears.

I took a deep breath. I began to question whether or not I was cut out to be an assistant. But despite it, I ended up in Fab's white Escalade with Shaq and Kev, another one of Fab's homies. We were headed to Jersey to get Fab's other outfit. In the truck I vented, loudly, becoming irate.

"His woman is a fuckin' stylist!" I yelled. "Why can't she bring him something? This is bullshit! I told his ass to bring two damn outfits!"

I was going off. Little did I know, during my rant Fab had called Shaq. Fab was listening to me the entire time. I didn't realize it until Shaq handed me the phone. We immediately began to argue again. This time, I remembered Skip's words..."You don't need that job. I'll take care of you."

Those words played over and over in my mind. They drowned out Fab. It was then that I made my decision. Hanging up on Fab, I asked Shaq to drop me off on 34th Street. I hopped out, went about my way and never looked back.

That same night, Cheo called me and asked if I would attend a special dinner that was being thrown for Fab to celebrate the release of his album. "Winter, you need to come," he said. "Your work went a long way in making this happen. It's going to look funny if you don't show up."

I didn't give a fuck how it would look. I declined and expected that everything would blow over in a few days. It didn't. Cheo called me again the next day. "Hey, I spoke to Fab," he said. "He told me to tell you all you have to do is apologize for talking shit about him and you can have your job back."

Nigga please, I thought to myself. I wish I would. Besides, Skip wasn't having it even if I decided to go back. He was now calling me his girl. The first time he said it, it gave me goose bumps. I wasn't ready to fall in love…but I needed security while I found a new job.

Eventually Fab and I spoke again a few weeks later. He strongly felt I was wrong for talking shit about him in the truck. I explained to him that I was fed up with how I was being treated. I also reminded him that I had gone above and beyond what my responsibilities were to him. I'd done things that weren't even in the job description and never got acknowledged for it. Fab knew it was true and understood my feelings. We ended our conversation on a good note and I told him that if he ever needed me, I would always be around.

That wouldn't change.

All I kept thinking about was that video. Yeah, I made him better.

Nothing but love for Fabolous.

19   Mama, I Got Me A Balla

My new life with Skip felt like a ghetto fairy tale. Since it was the off season, we were able to spend every moment together and truly get to know one another. He didn't have any pressing schedules nor did I. It was just us two against the world hanging out, partying, and mingling with friends. Through him I met his friend JR and Skip got cool with my girls, Chrissy, Ebony and Chynae.

Everything seemed perfect. We were truly playing house. I was cooking for him, nourishing his body while he took care of my mental. We shopped together and cuddled on the couch watching movies together like we were married. Everything was so cool that when his birthday rolled around that July, I decided to throw him a party. I invited a few of our closest friends, including Chrissy, Ebony, Chynae, and Raheem. Raheem was my neighbor and we'd become close so I valued his opinion coming from a male about what to do for Skip. We surprised him with a beautiful cake that had the number of his jersey written across it— 11. That was also the day I gave him the key to my apartment.

Skip was really my man. It felt weird to finally be able to say that and know it was true. I had never given any man

besides Smiley my time like I was giving Skip. He felt the
same way, bragging to his friends that he was giving me
good loving; "Tearing my ass up every night," as he would
say. I laughed it off. It was funny. And so untrue.

Yet, being with Skip felt like a huge weight had been
lifted off of my shoulders. Without Fab's demands, I felt
free. I was free to focus on building a relationship. I was free
to be happy. It was amazing. It was like a whole new life.
There was only one thing that made things very shaky between us. It was a problem that no one would have ever
guessed. I chose to keep it a secret from everyone except my
closest friends because it would make Skip look sketchy.

That same problem sent me backsliding. Seriously, I
did make a strong attempt at being faithful to Skip. We were
a month into our relationship and I was struggling to keep
things one hundred with him. In my defense, the whole being
faithful concept was kind of new to me. I was used to being
free. Cutting my past ways loose was like quitting crack cold
turkey. That's why when Young Berg called out of nowhere
and asked me to come see him, the shit was like dangling
raw meat in front of a pit bull. I knew I shouldn't have accepted. I knew what would most likely go down. But, being
faithful was something I struggled with.

I headed downtown to meet Young Berg at his hotel
room in Times Square. He was in town to do a performance
at The Lime Light in Manhattan. I'd first met Young Berg
just a few months prior. I was with Chrissy one day when
she needed to drop off some clothes to Jimmy at the "Sexy
Lady" video shoot. Jimmy was being featured in the video. I
was introduced to Berg and we both knew immediately there
was chemistry between us. It was strange because he was ten
years younger than me. I'd never fooled with a man that
young. Later on, because of our age difference, he began to
call me his "Old Head".

Nevertheless, since the chemistry was there, we talked

166

and eventually exchanged numbers. Afterward, we talked pretty often once he went back to his hometown in Chicago. A lot of the conversations led to us talking about eventually getting together to mess around. Of course, I kept the conversations secret from Skip. I didn't want to jack up a good thing. But despite not wanting to take a chance on hurting what Skip and I were building, I still found myself in Young Berg's hotel room. I felt guilty in the beginning but it eventually faded.

As we chilled, I loved staring at such a young, beautiful specimen of a man. His youth turned me on. I loved his boyish looks, his smile, his pretty eyes, his small frame. He was cute. He also had a nice swagger and rocked it well. Shit, I wanted to fuck him right then and there. I can't lie about it. I was mad curious to see if his little ass could handle a woman like me, especially after all the shit he'd been talking to me during our phone conversations. I truly had plans to turn him out. I quickly found out though that I'd underestimated him.

That little dude was a full blown beast in bed. What I liked about his sex game most was that he took his time. He didn't just climb in and start roughing me off. He gave me excellent foreplay filled with soft kisses and caresses. He tasted my body, enjoying it like he was eating a meal. I was surprised by his performance. I would've never expected that from someone so young. I was also surprised by his size. I mean, Berg had a huge package and knew exactly how to use it. On top of all that, he was long lasting too. He reminded me of the Energizer Bunny. In the end, he had me sucking wind.

Despite that slip up, I tried to make my relationship work with Skip. But just two months into the relationship, we faced another problem. In August of that year, Skip got into a fight with another man at a New York nightclub. During the fight, someone from Skip's crew slashed the man's neck. We had no idea how much trouble that incident would cause him until his lawyer called and told him to turn himself in. That ordeal turned out to be a nightmare. Afterwards, Skip's lawyers assured him the situation would play itself out and there would be no heavy consequences. But the Houston Rockets had something to say about it. They had him fly back to Texas immediately. That fight initiated another chapter in my life.

When Skip returned to Houston he said he was sure the Rockets were going to trade him. He told me about all the trade rumors that had been swirling around. Some information came from his teammates, and other times it was from more reputable sources. It was at that point I learned much more about Skip than I'd expected. He told me that the team considered him a trouble maker. In the past, he'd had some issues and had now developed a reputation for being the initiator of problems. The team had begun to think he didn't know how to disconnect his past life in the streets from the one the NBA now provided. They were basically fed up.

Shortly after our initial talk, he called me and said, "Winter, I'm being traded to Orlando. I want you to come with me."

I was stunned that he would want me with him. I couldn't believe it.

"I really want you with me," he continued. "I promise I'll take care of you."

I told him that was a serious move. I'd only known him less than three months. I needed time to think about it. He said okay and we hung up. I spoke to Chrissy about it, definitely needing some of her advice. She was pretty much batting a thousand up until that point so I took her words for the gospel at that time.

"Girl do it," she said. "Put your all into him. Make that relationship work."

After talking to Chrissy, I sat alone and thought back

on my life. I saw all the faces: Smiley, Nino, Big Money, Dame Dash, etc, etc. I thought about old memories, friendships and emotions. I thought about everything that had affected my heart. Everything that had made me laugh and cry. I thought about how many times I'd played and had *been* played. It all overwhelmed me. It had all been done and experienced in a search for happiness.

Even though I talked a good game about not wanting to be tied down and showing little emotions, a part of me wanted to finally settle down. The realization shone through like a bright, blinding light. This was the moment I'd been waiting for all my life. I'd finally found what I was looking for. With Skip, I now had stability, money, someone who truly cared for me, and a future. I no longer had to work from sun up to sun down. I no longer had to hustle or look for my next meal ticket. I now had the chance to be treated like the queen I'd always dreamed of. The world was finally mine.

I did it.

I decided to move over a thousand miles away from home to be with my man. I didn't look back. I planned to settle in with Skip like he'd done with me. I planned for our feelings to grow deeper than before. I truly wanted it to work. There was one problem though. I wanted to show him how much I appreciated him in that one special way every woman wants to show her man she cared for him...

I wanted to whip it on him!

After yet another denial, I couldn't hold the fact that we'd never been sexual with one another a secret any longer. Even though Ebony, Chrissy and Chynae knew that Skip and I never screwed, I hoped that maybe Raheem or one of Skip's boys would provide some sort of explanation from a male perspective. It wasn't like I was holding the pussy hostage. He was my man so I was throwing it at him every chance I got, especially after a night of drinking. Just like any other hormonal woman, when I got liquor in my system I wanted to get butt naked and work out like a beast. But for some reason, Skip didn't. I didn't know what the problem was. Damn near every time Ebony would see me after that, she would ask, "Did y'all do it yet?" There were always jokes coming from her along with my other friends. Somehow I found it funny, too.

When I would ask Skip what was up, he just told me he respected me and wanted to wait. I accepted that but I remained horny. I dealt with it, anxiously waiting, wondering what it would finally be like to get the real thing. September of that year rolled around. I had packed my clothes but left everything else and moved to Orlando with my mother. Skip hadn't got there yet but he paid for everything. The move excited me. My future excited me. I could see myself sitting in the sky boxes with the other NBA wives as my husband balled up and down the court. I couldn't wait to see what that experience would be like.

Everything started out well. While in Orlando I had a chance to bond with my mother and stepfather. I also had a brother in his teens that I had only seen maybe nine or ten times out of my entire life. I enjoyed getting a chance to build a relationship with him. Seeing him mature and learning about his personality intrigued me, and I realized I'd missed out on so much family time.

I hadn't lived with Jackie since I was 12 years old, although I stayed with her off and on until she married my stepfather when I was 11 and moved to the Poconos. Since then we hadn't spent a whole lot of time together. Now we were getting a chance to make up for lost time. I found out we were both reading the book, "The Secret" when I told her my plan to be married soon and have a child shortly thereafter. My mother's response was, "Winter, when your gut tells you something, that's God talking so listen."

Just watching her mannerisms and hearing her voice

when she reacted to certain situations did something to me. Through watching her I learned a lot about myself. Plus her wisdom was more than what I expected to obtain while in Orlando. Through my mother, I matured in a short period of time.

The move was a drastic change for me but obviously a good one. And as I look back, it was the slowest point of my life for the past ten years. I was finally able to relax and do things normal people do. Instead of always watching the clock and having to answer my phone, I was able to sit in the nail salon and enjoy a pedicure and manicure. I was able to cook dinner with my mom and gossip. I was able to sit on the couch and watch television and sometimes we'd even shop until we dropped, since Skip regularly sent me five thousand a month. Damn, it felt good.

My mom and I also talked a lot. She even told me how she felt when Fab got shot.

"I wanted you gone from there," she said. "That wasn't the place for you if the person you worked for got people shooting at him."

I asked her if she'd forgotten how strong of a female I was. I'm different than most. She just shook her head.

Although I loved catching up on my relationship with my family, I missed Skip. Somehow he was still on The Houston Rocket's roster. Neither of us knew why, or maybe he did and just wasn't telling me. Also, Orlando was extremely lame. I was getting bored out of my mind, especially now that I had so much time on my hands. And as the old saying goes; "Idle hands are the devil's workshop." When I wasn't with my family, I was sneaking back and forth to Miami at least three nights a week where I kicked it with Alyah an old flame of Fab's who lived there. Yeah, it was wrong but I needed some sense of normalcy. I wasn't seeing Skip a lot, other than when The Rockets played The Magic or the Heat. Our relationship had dwindled down to spending most of our time on the phone other than those few times we'd meet up. Still, no sex.

In November Skip began to work with developers in Miami on a new condo community at the W Hotel on South Beach where he was buying a condo as an investment property. I drove from Orlando to meet him. I couldn't wait to see him. But shortly after I arrived, we got some bad news from the developer.

"Mr. Alston, the property won't be ready until March of 08," he stated.

I was disappointed to say the least. March was four months away. There was no way I could take staying in Orlando and being bored to death for that long. I could continue to sneak back and forth to Miami but I knew Skip would find out if I kept doing it. He wouldn't have approved of it.

Damn, I didn't want to stay in Orlando any longer than I had to. I mean kicking it with my family was cool and everything but I needed a life. I guess I'd grown so used to the limelight that I was starting to miss it; at least some of it. I seriously thought about going back to New York but Chrissy had told me she'd already rented my old place out since I had claimed Florida as my new home.

All types of crazy thoughts started swirling inside my head. I wished my new life and relationship would backfire. The boredom was killing me that badly. I couldn't believe that I'd moved hundreds of miles away from home for a man I was barely getting to see and I couldn't even get any sex from. We had been together at that point for six months and still no damn sex. What man goes that long without pussy? I dealt with it though.

Anyway, a new year finally dragged its way around. 2008 came and I was growing tired of our long distance relationship. I was also growing tired of sneaking back and forth to Miami but I refused to stop. Shit, Miami was where everything was. Sad to say, it was also where I began fooling around behind Skip's back. He was a Jamaican. I met him in a club one night. I fell for his accent and explained to him that I was in a relationship, still our relationship took off quickly and my lies to Skip became more frequent. I also began hanging out with Dorell Wright of The Miami Heat. It was nothing serious though; we were just chilling.

I felt bad for cheating on Skip. Truly I did, but the long distance thing just wasn't cutting it with me. My body and soul needed some attention. Skip wasn't giving me neither. What did he want me to do? Wait on him? I had needs, but I held on.

I saw Pecas at Wet Willies. He was head of promotions for Fab's projects when I worked for him so he and I had history. The timing was perfect. He told me he had heard I was messing with a ball player, frowning about it the entire time. I played it off like everything was good, not wanting to put my personal business out there. Immediately, I let him know I was interested in getting back in the industry. He agreed and suggested that I work on building my resume more.

"Yeah, I know you're used to having your own," he said. "I can hook you up with Ted Lucas over at Slip-N-Slide Records."

At that time, Slip-N-Slide wasn't popping like Roc-A-Fella or Bad Boy. They only had Trina and Plies. Rick Ross was there and beginning to bubble but he was nowhere near the huge success he now is. I was still grateful though. Anything would be better than nothing. I just needed to get back in the swing of things before I went crazy.

I really did miss the business. I missed the lights. I missed it all. Being with Skip showed me that. My life somehow had become super boring and too damn predictable. There was no excitement and no surprises. I realized that I'd gotten with Skip because I was at a vulnerable point in my life. I was tired of the game. But that was *then*. This was *now*.

Anyway, just like he'd said, Pecas hooked me up with Ted Lucas. I found myself sitting with him at Olive's on South Beach, expecting some country dude with dreads, gold teeth and his pants hanging off his ass. Or maybe even a nigga who favored Trick Daddy, since at that time a lot of people thought Trick Daddy owned the label. My expectations turned out to be all the way off the mark. Ted Lucas was tall, handsome and well mannered. He spoke properly and professionally. He definitely wasn't what I expected of a Hip Hop CEO—nothing I'd seen since Dame.

Ted asked me about myself and my experience. I told him about my job with Fab and let him know that was how I knew Pecas. I also ran down the long list of people and companies for which I'd worked. He seemed impressed and wanted to know more. I explained to him why I had moved to Orlando, had begun spending a lot of time in Miami, and gave him a little info about my relationship with Skip. I told him that the job would have to be a secret because he didn't really want me working in the industry. I let him know that although being the girl of an NBA player was cool, I needed my own. I wasn't used to being a housewife. Ted understood. The two of us talked for nearly an hour. When we were done, he said he hadn't made a decision yet about the job but he would let me know soon.

That Monday morning Ted called me and told me to stop by the office, which was located on South Beach. Tiana, a friend of mine from New York was hanging out with me at the time. I headed over to the office to meet with Ted. When I got there, he told me his assistant had quit that very morning. And instead of looking for an office manager, he was now looking for an assistant.

My experience with Fab had intrigued Ted. During the interview back at Olive's, I had explained my duties for Fab in detail. I'd told him all the extremes. He knew that I would be able to fit perfectly. He wanted me to start that Monday morning. That meant I would have to find a place in Miami and get settled. No more driving back and forth from Orlando. I was now an official Miami resident.

Just like that, I was Ted's assistant. Immediately, I discovered it was nothing like the job I had with Fab. There were no toting guns, no strip clubs, no buying weed, no hanging out in the studio. It was all professional and legitimate. The pay wasn't that good but it was much more than what Fab had paid.

The day I started, Trina's album had just been released a few weeks prior so I jumped in immediately. Just like every job before that one, I worked hard and went the extra mile. At Slip-N-Slide I was beginning to learn the mechanics of the business and running a label. I worked on artist's agreements, scheduled hair and make up for the artists, paid their stylist and anyone else who needed to be paid. I was even learning exactly *how* to get the artists on the radio. At every other job, working with the artist, we just showed up at the station ready to get on the air. With Slip-N-Slide I learned what led up to it. I also learned what it really took from a label's view to promote an artist or album, where as before, we just spent the label's money. I felt like I had truly arrived.

The experience intrigued me. Ted was taking me under his wing and teaching me so much that I had never known about this game. He was showing me the other side of the music industry. An exceptional business man, he wasn't too crazy about the spotlight. He could do without it. As I said before, a lot of people thought Trick Daddy owned the label. That was fine with Ted. It allowed him to stay behind the scenes and handle business.

Of all the CEO's I've come across in the industry, by far Ted was the most interesting. I mean, this cat was so different from anyone I'd met before or since. There were no e-mails or texts coming to him from other women. He didn't hang out and party. He didn't pop pills or smoke weed. This cat was just unreal. I had never known men like him existed. My admiration grew.

A new side of the industry wasn't the only thing Ted brought into my life. He also brought God into my life in a way that changed me. After working with him for just two weeks, he invited me to church with him and his family. I'd been to church with Chrissy and Raheem back in Harlem a few times so I missed going. I took Ted up on his offer. The experience brought something out of me.

While sitting in church, I started crying and couldn't stop. I didn't know why. I did know, though, that maybe it was time to reevaluate my life. Also, maybe it was time to start going to God for help and advice instead of my girls. When I left that day, I saw my relationship with God a lot differently than before.

From that point, I began praying to God and talking to him much more often. I needed guidance for the future and I had faith he'd provide it. Honestly, I looked back on my life and didn't like what I saw or who I'd let myself become. I really wanted to be a better human being. I really wanted to be the best Winter I could be. I started going to church regularly and even got baptized. If I didn't show up for church, Ted would text me immediately. I swear, it was like he was retraining me on life. He was just that influential. I'll forever be grateful to him for that.

Church and Miami changed me a lot. I finally realized it was time to leave the past in the past. The selfish person I'd been back in New York needed to stay back there. With Miami as my new home, I now had a chance to open a new chapter of my life and write it much better than the previous one. I was focused on it. Sadly though, as God had entered my life, someone else was about to be excluded from it.

Eventually, summer rolled around. In July of 08 Skip and I went to Vegas for his birthday. His daughter accompanied us too. The three of us stayed at the Luxor Hotel. We were there for three to four days. Skip sponsored an AAU team there so we attended a few of their games, spending time together. We also did a lot of shopping, including me taking his daughter to Lens Crafters to get herself a new pair of glasses. Of course Skip took me shopping too, ending with the comment, "This is the first time I ever bought a woman a bag besides my mother."

Whatever, I thought.

The next night, we decided to leave Skip's daughter in the hotel room and go out. We hit the club. While there, I bumped into Angie Martinez. The two of us chatted for a moment. I also saw Pecas. We spoke. Then out of nowhere I got the scare of my life. My heart jumped into my throat when I saw who walked in the door.

It was Dwyane Wade.

Dwyane was there with Gabrielle. I wasn't sure if he knew about me. I wasn't sure if Dorell had told him about me or by chance had showed him some pictures of us. Panicked filled me as I wondered if my cover was about to be blown. Thank God it wasn't. Dwayne didn't know my face, at least not at that time. The night ended up running smoothly with Skip and I enjoying ourselves. Deep inside, I kept my fingers crossed about how things would go down once we got back to the room.

Skip and I headed back to the Luxor. His daughter was asleep when we got there so I decided to make a move on Skip tearing at his pants. He was drunk so my hope was to take advantage of him. Quickly, he turned me down.

"We've been here for two days," I told him. "It's your birthday and we're coming up on our one year anniversary. Can I get some sex?"

Once again, he turned me down.

"Not tonight, baby. I want us to wait. When we do it, I want it to be special."

I couldn't believe this dude. Was he fuckin' serious? Something wasn't right, I accepted at that point. Men just don't turn down ass. Something was definitely wrong with that picture. Either he was getting major ass from another chick or....

Maybe he wasn't that into me.

20   Another Season

The seasons changed again.

By Fall Skip had slowed down on the money he was sending me. For the entire time I'd been in Orlando he'd been sending me stacks every month faithfully. But all of a sudden, once he found out I'd been working at Slip-N-Slide he began sending less money and hadn't given me a reason. The nigga had downsized me. It didn't make sense. First he wanted to deprive me of dick. Now he wanted to play games with the money. What in the hell was up with him? Rather than dwell on it, I just realized I had to do me and get back on my grind.

Christmas of that year rolled around. Everything at Slip-N-Slide was going good. I decided to ask Skip for a car so I could get around better. I'd already picked out the one I wanted and was sure he would get it for me. Although he'd fell back on the five thousand dollars every month, I was still able to get money from him freely. He surprised me though when I asked for the BMW. He told me 'no' and offered no explanation. It was at that point I knew we were over. We were still in a long distance relationship, but his phone calls to me were even growing fewer and fewer. Now I couldn't have a car? What was the use in being together? I tried to stick it out though. I really did.

Journal Entry

My mother could never understand the shit I go through with Skip. My step father treats her like a queen. No worries of other women, spending enough time together- nothing. I never see him- wondering if there is another bitch. How did I end up in this kind of situation when my step-dad is nothing like this man. Should a woman want to be with a man like her father especially if he's a loving,caring and providing man? I guess I need to reevaluate my situation and get me a white man. Shit- rewind- I doubt that -I'm hooked on the brothers. I wish I could duplicate my step dad though and marry him- everything would be all better. Maybe if I drop this loser that good man will be waiting. Maybe I should find this good man first then drop the loser just in case.

Valentine's Day 2009. It was that day that I discovered Skip was finally being traded to Orlando. He texted me saying, he was on his way to Orlando and for me to meet him there. At that moment I realized it was time to come clean about my secrets. I was still fooling with the Jamaican dude and also dating Dorell from The Miami Heat. Obviously, there was no way Skip would be able to live just four hours from Miami and not find out. I had to tell him. I owed him that. Plus, I was ready for the relationship to be over.

I went to meet Skip and told him it was over. I told him about my relationship with Dorell…well not exactly.

"I've been messing with someone who plays for the Heat," I admitted.

"Who?" he asked nonchalantly. "Is it somebody I know?"

I told him it was none of his business. He was hurt of course and the relationship ended. Strangely, there was no yelling or screaming. I assumed it was because he was doing his own thing anyway. But one bizarre thing came out of it... We finally had sex. Damn, I'd waited for what seemed like forever. Now, he was giving it to me on the night we're breaking up? It was crazy. The only thing crazier though was quickly discovering what I'd been waiting for all that time really wasn't worth waiting for at all. The sex was a huge disappointment. It was horrible. Wow, so not worth the damn wait.

Back on my grind at Slip-N-Slide things moved at a rapid pace. Ted learned that a good friend of his, Shakir, shot and killed himself. My heart nearly dropped to my shoes after hearing the news. I couldn't believe it. I had a million questions, wondering why he would take his own life. I'd heard the rumors about what had possibly gone on...but knew nothing factual. The entire situation truly affected me. I immediately went into prayer. I knew a lot of men in the industry who had as much if not more pressure than Shakir. That situation taught me to get my shit together. I vowed to live life to the fullest and work was first on my agenda.

After that whole ordeal I approached Ted and asked for more responsibilities within the company. I knew I was destined to be more than an assistant. Although working with Fab had given me experiences most will never have in their lifetime, I needed more. Eventually Ted gave me what I needed.

A chance.

An opportunity.

He had a new artist named Shonie who he was trying to shop to a major record label. He gave me full responsibility over her project: wardrobe, radio, street team, promo tours etc. I put my best foot forward and started working with Shonie on a regular basis, putting my all into her. I was still Ted's assistant so I had my plate full, working crazy hours,

181

learning more and more about the business.

Journal Entry

Ted finally came to his senses and gave me Shonie. I'm ready. I like her and I think she can be really big in the industry. But of course no extra pay and added work. The story of my life but I'm ready to handle the responsibility and show what I can do. I'm sure I'll have to call in favors from my people in the industry but shit what else do I know them for and after all the shit I've done for them it's time to call in the favors. I've never been the one to shy away from a challenge and I'll take this one head on. I can't let Ted down he's taught me so much and I owe him for that. I think God put me in this position to show my talent and skills and I'm going to go super hard and get Shonie signed. From this day forward I will eat, sleep and shit Shonie making her top dog at Slip-N-Slide.

Shonie had a record Ted wanted to record but we needed a rapper to seal the deal. Being the fast-paced thinker that I am, I quickly came up with a few artists I could reach out to. Fabolous entered my mind instantly and ultimately became the label's unanimous decision. So I reached out to Fab and negotiated a fee—the family discount. Before long, I was sending parts of the record to Fab to add his verse. The fast pace in which he sent things back and the discount gave me props at Slip-N-Slide and improved our relationship.

I felt good about what I'd accomplished. All of my work, time and energy with Fab back in 2007 had not been in vain. And I had gotten the opportunity to show that I could build an artist.

Not long after Fab completed the record we worked hard at getting Shonie ready to head to New York to meet with L.A. Reid at Def Jam. I remember dressing her like she'd never been dressed before. A hair stylist and make-up artist were brought in to make things perfect. The record was so hot that I knew she'd come back to Miami with a deal. Shonie performed a few tracks for Mr. Reid and finally performed, "Can't Let Go", featuring Fabolous. It just so happened, record producer and song writer The-Dream was in the building and walked in on the meeting. He and L.A. loved the record and her energy. They had also heard Shonie and Fab's record on one of the New York radio stations. I had reached out to all my DJ homies in NY so the song played regularly on the radio.

Shonie came back to Miami with a major record deal with Def Jam Records. I was so excited about that accomplishment and proud that I was a large part of making it all happen. That solidified for me what Ted had been preaching all along, about believing in myself and working hard. I was ready to go full force with Shonie, but little did I know Ted was in the process of hiring a new head of Marketing, Randy Acker, someone who I'd never known to do marketing at a label.

It was crazy how it all happened. He came in at a rapid pace, making changes, some that were called for and some that were not. Of course I flipped when he decided to take control of Shonie's project. I thought it was a bad idea, but it wasn't my company so I wished Randy the best and fell back. In exchange, I was given the newly signed group Jagged Edge to work with.

I was super excited to work with Jagged Edge. They'd been in the business for several years and I'd always been a huge fan. My senses and new skills in the industry told me they could make a comeback. I wanted to be a part of it. Jagged Edge wasn't as easy to work with as I thought. The guys were easy to get along with but their management was just down right ridiculous. They were stuck in a time warp. They were expecting to get what the group got when they were selling millions of records.

I understood they were well known and they'd made some of the best R&B music ever, but that time had passed. They had to prove themselves all over again; sort of like starting off as a new artist. Not to mention, Ted was not going to go broke trying to make them feel like they were still with Jermaine Dupri. Ted was a smart businessman unlike others around him.

Journal Entry

I swear this industry is all smoke and mirrors. You drive a nice car, come up in here with thousands of dollars in jewelry, expensive ass clothes but the sheriff comes to the office looking for you about some shit you owe? I get it- you have to look nice for the camera but bitch when the cameras aren't rolling how about you pay your bills? Use some of that multi million dollar contract to get that debt taken care of. This must be serious though for the sheriffs to come here looking for you. I wonder how much I could get from world star or YBF if I leaked the story? Just kidding I wouldn't do that. Or would I? Bottom line is… stop frontin' and pay your bills. It's easy just hire an accountant. Do you even know what that is?

After a few months I sensed that Ted wasn't happy with the attitude and behavior of the group. They weren't showing up at events, missing studio time, and just weren't living up to their part of the deal. Eventually Ted stopped focusing on them, hoping they'd realize they were missing out on an opportunity so they would get their shit together. In the process of that the label wasn't bringing in any money. Trina was spending, and Rick Ross and Plies' checks were few and far between. Life became stressful again….and there was lots of pressure. I'd gone back to the days where I had to grind, hard. Extremely hard.

This time, I had Ted in my life and knew to pray about it.

21   Back To Business

As corny as it may sound, our eyes gazed into one another's across the small table like we were lovers. How he
managed to snag me, I still wasn't quite sure. Obviously, he
was minor compared to the dudes I was accustomed to. People knew I did only athletes or movers and shakers in the Hip
Hop world. Roc was neither. Thank God. The only thing he
had that resembled them was long money, although he was
infamous in a way that I can't say for now.

We'd met a few weeks prior in Vegas. My first thought
when I saw him at the Cheesecake Factory was not to give
him my number. Then I thought, why not try normal and average? I'd been involved in the bullshit of the entertainment
industry for so long that maybe I wanted to see if things
could be more realistic and stable with someone who was
just a regular person. The only problem, though, Roc was
still in a relationship with someone else; one he'd said had
gotten old. Words like that were common for me since I'd
been dealing with trained liars for years. That's the main reason why to this day I can't believe I fell for this dude. My
life had really changed.

We were chilling on South Beach having lunch. It

was a gorgeous day with the sun beaming, waves rushing. Women strolled in little to no clothing while couples held hands. It was exactly the atmosphere I'd moved to Miami for in the first place.

"So, what are we really doing?" I asked Roc, needing to know exactly what he wanted out of our three week old relationship. I'd been through enough games that men play and was tired of it. I was too grown now. I wanted him to be straight up.

"Look, you know I'm in this situation right now," he said.

I had to sigh at that one and took a sip of my drink. It sounded so much like Swizz. Although I already knew his situation, something about hearing it come from his mouth disappointed me. I was no longer okay with sharing my men. There would be no more playing second base. I thought back to the day when Smiley's other chick rolled up on us looking way better than me. I was done with that life.

Seeing my change in demeanor, he reached across the table, grabbed my hand and said, "I'm just trying to separate myself from her with the least amount of problems as possible. In the meantime, Winter, you know I like you. I want you with me."

He was so sexy to me: the look and feel of his beard, the way he spoke. It all turned me on, especially since his money was right. But it was countered by the game he was trying to run on me. Older and wiser, I understood when men were trying to have their cake and eat it too.

"So, what are you saying?" I asked needing him to be completely clear about us, although I knew in my heart I was playing with fire.

"I'm saying I'm breaking it off with her."

"When?"

"Soon."

Soon… meant game. I'd never ridden the short bus to

school when I was a kid. I wasn't slow at all. And especially not in 2010 at thirty-one years old. If he truly wanted to break it off, all it took was a phone call. Yet, instead of getting mad, I decided to go after what I felt would be in my best interest.

A Sugar Daddy.

I grinned, realizing how I'd play things until I figured out if he was being truthful about his situation. "So while you're handling that, what are you going to do for me to make me want to be yours? Assuming you'll end things quickly," I added. I felt like both Dame and Swizz's business sense were now guiding me.

"I'll take care of you."

That sounded good to my ears....but I wanted no more drama. Although I was still full time at Slip-N-Slide his proposition would give me a little more money, which meant more stability, especially if I played my cards correctly. So there would be no misunderstandings of what I needed, I reminded Roc of how expensively I was catered to when I was with Skip.

"I got you," Roc said as if it were no problem. "I just want you with me."

It was on. We were a couple. Even though he lived in Jersey and me in Miami. Deal- signed, sealed, and delivered. From that day on, things began to move quickly between us. Thankfully so because my love life had been in the dumps for a while.

Feelings began to stir deeply inside me. They seemed to be more extreme than before. I remember praying that they didn't get to the level of emotions that I felt for Big Money. I was now afraid to go back there...but a part of me began to wonder if the feelings were moving towards love, but knowing myself, that wasn't the case. Big Money messed me up that badly. Still, though, I was spending every weekend in Jersey. I was even doing little catty shit like leaving clothes and shoes behind to mark my territory, just in case there were some chicks coming around I didn't know about. Eventually, he was feeling me so much that he intro- duced me to his mother. His mother and I hit it off and spent countless hours together, shopping, going to dinner and just hanging out at Roc's house drinking wine and cooking out. They felt like family even though they weren't my blood. As time went on Roc and I talked about having our own family since my feelings for him were growing deep. I really wanted to have a baby, someone I could nurture, love and take care of. My age was becoming a factor for me although under forty, while older women around me were talking about freezing their eggs. That type of talk made me try to get pregnant even more.

Roc was a good candidate for a father since I'd seen the way he catered to his daughter who lived in North Car- olina and the relationship he had with his mother. I'd even gotten his name tattooed on my stomach...ROC...written with fancy letters. That's how much I wanted to snag him and keep him under lock. I now realize that tattoo was a bad move. I wouldn't advise any female to do that since you never know how life can take a sudden turn. I still have that tattoo today—with slight alterations. Meanwhile I wanted for nothing.

Journal Entry

Trying to get pregnant. What else can I do?
Prayed about it- keep trying too. Nothing.

Just as he'd agreed, Roc took good care of me, not al- lowing me to want for anything; not even allowing any of my bills to go unpaid. The main difference between him and others—he took care of me mentally.

At first.

Most of us know that when something seems too good

to be true, something bad happens. Instead of things falling through with Roc, my career took a sudden turn. In August I got that call, the one all grown-ups hate. Randy asked if I would mind working for free for a few months until the label was back on track.

"Hell no," I said. I was not ok with that. I felt like Randy came in, spent a ton of Ted's money with very little to show for it and now he wanted me to work for free. *Fuck out of here*, I thought. Although I was grateful for all Ted had done for me I couldn't work for free.

Then Randy made a statement that pissed me off. "You need to grind like everybody else."

I let loose on Randy. I had to remind him I was the one who got Shonie the deal at Def Jam. Upset, I decided to keep it moving, not wanting to bring any drama to Ted's label. Onto the next project. Of course I ended up back in Jersey with Roc for one of our planned weekends together. At least with him there was stability.

Or so I thought.

One night after dinner at a lavish restaurant we were heading back to his house. As Roc drove, he began to pay close attention to his rearview. I could sense something was wrong.

"Baby, what's up?" I asked.

Roc didn't answer. He just kept glancing in the rear view, causing me to do the same. All I could see were headlights. Roc busted a quick right onto a side street.

"Baby, what's up? Where are we going?"

Something definitely wasn't right. Ignoring me, Roc sped up slightly. I looked in the rearview just in time to see the head lights of a car quickly turn onto the side street right behind us. Approaching Roc's bumper, its head lights began to flood the interior of our car.

"Roc, what the hell is going on?" I asked him frantically.

Ignoring me, Roc slammed on the gas pedal so hard my back slammed against my seat. Within a fraction of a moment, I knew we were up to at least sixty miles per hour. What the fuck had he gotten us into? I wondered. My thoughts were going a mile a minute. Were there drug dealers behind us? Had Roc crossed someone? Did he owe someone some damn money?

"Roc, who's behind us?"

Without saying a word, he skidded onto a busy street.

Before I knew it, he busted another quick turn onto a side street. We were on a one way going in the wrong direction, causing cars to skid out. The sounds of the brakes screeching loudly as they avoided us by only inches had me going wild.

"Roc, stop it! Stop *now*! Let me out!"

Roc's cell phone rang, sitting underneath the center console. He glanced down at it but didn't answer. He was completely focused on dodging the oncoming traffic, while continuing to glance in the rearview every now and then. After several rings, the cell stopped. Common sense told me the person who was calling was the chaser.

We were going so fast and dodging so many cars I was scared to death. I mean, I almost literally pissed on myself. All I could see in my mind was us running head on into someone's car and flying through the windshield. Soon, the cell phone rang again. Roc didn't even look at it this time. We reached the end of the one way and skidded onto another busy street so hard the force almost threw me completely into the driver's seat with Roc. He dipped and swerved in and out of traffic. Then after a few quick rights and lefts, he looked into the rearview and slowed down relieved.

"Fool, what the hell is wrong with you?" I screamed angrily as we entered Garden State Parkway. "You could've killed us back there! Are you crazy?"

A strange look spread across Roc's face, a stress filled

one. He looked at me almost pitifully. "That was my girl chasing us," he finally admitted.

That one took me all the way by surprise. It took me back to when Dame had the girl in the car. At that moment I realized nothing had really changed in my life.

"I thought you said you and her were done?" I blasted.

Well, he never verbally told me she was officially gone but his actions showed me she was definitely out the picture. I assumed he'd gotten rid of his old chick since she never called his house the many times I stayed there. Guess I was wrong. I felt like I had to go in full "I'ma get you back mode." At the time I wasn't sure what needed to be done. Friends later told me I was crazy for never asking questions about him ending it with his chick. I guess I didn't want to really know. The relationship seemed genuine and I didn't want to lose it.

The two of us grew silent as he drove home. I was seething. He'd made me look like an idiot. All this time, I'd thought he was different from the rest. Come to find out he was just as much about games as every other man I'd been with. Although angry, I let things die down, vowing to hang in the relationship, but now just for the money. The green always seemed to pull me back in.

I never spoke on it again, choosing to let it go. That was until one day while washing Roc's clothes, I found some wack ass cheap bloomer panties. Knowing they were hers and that he still hadn't let her go, I realized it was the last straw. My gut was speaking to me. God was trying to tell me something. I would no longer give him my all. I thought about calling it quits but figured since I didn't have a job I'd just keep him around a little longer. I vowed not to deal with another man who couldn't respect me and treat me right. I also came to the conclusion that if my relationships were going to work I needed to be straight up and committed too.

The Roc situation had me messed up but new light was

shed on my work situation. My phone rang early 2010 while at home in Miami. Raheem's voice said excitedly from the other end of the line, "Yo, Winter, you interested in taking a meeting with Slim from Cash Money?"

Immediately, I leaned forward in my chair, "Definitely, why?"

"I hooked it up for you."

"Are you serious?"

"Hell yeah."

The meeting was right on time. I definitely needed a pay check coming in after leaving Slip-N-Slide. The only money I had coming in at that moment was the change from Roc, but his infidelities weighed heavily on me. After discovering the panties in the laundry, I still hadn't forgiven him, although I had him believing I did. He'd never have my trust or my heart again. It was all about the money. But having my own steady income would definitely help me out.

"Alright," Raheem said. "He wants to meet you tonight at one o'clock."

"No problem," I told him.

A one o'clock meeting may sound suspect to most people. But actually, it's the norm in the Hip Hop world. Between touring, promoting, endorsements, and so much more, executives and artists have to squeeze meetings in wherever and whenever they can.

Raheem came back to my place so he and I could go to the meeting together. He'd been staying in Miami with me for a while making me think the sudden opportunity was meant to be. In blue jeans, red bottoms, wife beater and a vest, I climbed out of my BMW in front of a studio with which I was familiar. During my Murder Inc. and Fabolous days, I'd been here plenty of times.

"Hey, girl, where you been?" the receptionist asked me when I walked into the lobby.

"Just stayin' out the way."

The two of us chatted about old times. As she mentioned certain names and moments, I realized that I missed that world. It had been such a part of my life for so long. Raheem and I headed back to the waiting area to wait for Slim. Something on the flat screen television caught my attention. I was facing it and talking to Raheem about it when I heard Slim's heavily southern laced voice come from behind me. I turned around immediately.

I'm used to dealing with men. I'm used to talking to them. I'm never threatened by their presence, no matter how rich or how successful. But I swear something I'd never felt in my life came over me as I saw what seemed like a seven foot giant standing in front of me. The feeling couldn't be described. It seemed like a mixture of both nervousness and intimidation.

Slim wasn't just *anyone* in the Hip Hop game. He was a *somebody*. Slim owned fifty percent of Cash Money Records, one of the hottest labels in the game. With his younger brother Birdman, Slim had sold millions of albums and had made hundreds of millions of dollars. He was a true power player in the industry.

Politely, I extended my hand to him and thanked him for the meeting. He took my hand and gave me a small grin. The feel of his hand in mine sent another unexplainable feeling through me. Damn, what the fuck was happening to me? I mean, real talk, my pussy got moist. The shit was crazy!

Slim wasn't physically attractive to me at all. His complexion didn't have any sort of golden glow to it. His frame was lanky, instead of muscular. He didn't even have the cuts of an NBA player. His eyes were sort of bulging from their sockets. And as a mover and shaker in this industry, he didn't have the hulking and menacing presence of Suge Knight or the confidently cocky and charismatic character of Jay-Z. But something, *not* the money, had me drawn to him.

Slim, on the other hand, didn't show any interest in me.

His smile had been merely out of politeness. It was all business with him. I'm a bad bitch if I must say so myself, but obviously he'd been around bad bitches ever since the millions started rolling in. Women as beautiful as me came a dime a dozen in his world.

Slim and I spoke business for a few hours then just kicked it until about four a.m. By then, I was ready to go. My days of hanging out in the studio until sun up were done. Slim gave me his number and exchanged good byes with myself and Raheem. Just before we left, Slim advised me to read some book I can't remember the name of now. He said he had read it during a flight to Miami and that it made good reading while on his jet. The thought of being on his jet excited me but I didn't show it. I simply told him I'd get the book and kept it moving.

Over the next few nights, Slim continued to keep it all about business as we spoke on the phone several times. He inquired about my past work and experience in the industry. That always seemed to turn into me discussing things like why I'd moved to Miami, and who in the industry I'd dated. I kept it 100 with him, telling him the truth, knowing he probably knew the answers anyway. Gossip played a huge part in the industry. He didn't seem to look down on me, at least he didn't express it if he did. But I knew he considered me a gold digger. I didn't care though. All that mattered was being able to handle my duties as Slim's assistant.

Over the next few weeks, we talked more and more but he would never give me a direct answer about whether or not I had the job. It was starting to feel like he was stringing me along. Eventually, the weeks turned into a few months. Fed up, I finally gave him a salary offer. I needed to know what was up with the position. He brushed it off, once again not giving me a concrete answer. It was obvious then he was playing games. Either I had it or I didn't.

He wasn't trying to hire me.

22   Always Grindin'

I began to question why I allowed men to monopolize my time and energy. Although Slim had wasted my time, I continued to hang out with him. I don't quite know why. I mean, it didn't seem like he was going to hire me and he didn't seem interested in fucking me. I had no idea what was up.

While spending time with Slim, I got a chance to learn a lot about him; mainly that he was the complete opposite of what people would expect from a Hip Hop CEO. He was mature, didn't party, had no kids and preferred to stay low key and behind the scenes. Those things kind of turned me on about him. I mean, he was nowhere near as handsome as what I was used to but his personality and heart of gold made up for what he was lacking in the looks department. But despite feeling him, I couldn't do it anymore. Spending time with him was affecting things between me and Roc. And since Slim wasn't trying to give me the assistant position, I couldn't fuck up the money train I was riding with Roc. I had no choice but to fall back from Slim.

Not long after discovering the panties at Roc's, I got a call from my old roommate Tiana about a mutual friend, Lore'l, who was an aspiring rapper and who is now a cast member on Love and Hip Hop New York. I'd first met Lore'l in Miami a while back and took a liking to her. She had that same 'I don't give a fuck' attitude I had. She reminded me of myself; plus her rhyme skills were nice.

Anyway, Tiana said Lore'l needed financial help with her career. That's when I realized why I had kept Roc's lying ass around for so long after the car chase. *Money!* After discussing with Lore'l exactly what she needed, I presented it to Roc as a business opportunity that was sure to pay off due to my connections in the music industry. He went for it. From that point, he footed the bill on everything business related, including hotel rooms, promotions, and plane trips, with the expectation of getting a nice return on his investment when Lore'l's career finally took off.

NOT!

Just like he'd played me, I was going to play him back. Once Lore'l got on, I was going to toss Roc a few measly racks and send him on his way. I was done with love and I was done with liars!

I went back to focusing on my new protégé, Lore'l who was nice lyrically. The only problem was her personal life was mad fucked up. The way she went about things was backwards, especially regarding men, specifically famous athletes. She was more star struck than focusing on getting money out of them. She was pretty much fucking all these millionaires for free. I hated that about her.

At the time, Lore'l was signed to a good friend of mine, Red Café. Not wanting to step on his toes, I told him I was taking her under my wing. I really wanted to help her succeed.

Shaking his head, Red said, "Winter, working with her won't be an easy process. She ain't easy to work with, but good luck if that's what you want to do."

I told him I could handle it.

"If you say so," he told me. "But just remember I

warned you. She ain't what you think."

With that said, he walked away laughing like he knew something I didn't. His loud laugh still rings in my head to this day.

Thinking she couldn't be as bad as he'd made her out to be, I went on with my plans, knowing she had the talent to make it and as long as I put everything I had into her, she'd be loyal and appreciative. Besides, she was hungry and I wanted to help. Not to mention someone else was footing the bill and we'd all benefit.

I was on my grind again with Lore'l hoping for the same success I'd had with Shonie. We'd been grinding hard for about six months when I received a call from Slim out of the blue. I was working in Tampa so I made the call short. I hadn't meant to make it seem like I was shrugging him off, but my work had me busy at the moment so I told him I would get up with him when I got back to Miami.

Immediately after hanging up, just like the very first moment I'd met him, a strange feeling came over me. I realized that I had missed talking to him. I had missed his presence. It compelled me to text him back immediately.

Damn I miss talking to you. Can't wait to get back to Miami.

The very next morning, I was back in the MIA around ten. I called him a little later, hoping his schedule would permit him to see me. Thankfully, it did. We made plans to meet up at the studio. While there, I kicked it with both him and his driver. Once again, I brought up my salary offer.

Giving his driver a sideways look, Slim asked, "What you think, bruh? You think she's cut for the team?"

The driver glanced at me and returned Slim's look. Without answering the question, he simply laughed. I knew then I wasn't getting the job.

After a few more months went by of us not really keeping contact, I decided to call him.

"Your dude kicked you to the curb, huh, so you calling me now?" he asked without even saying "Hello".

Why would he care about my dude?

"You must like me or something if you're questioning me about him," I said. "Just say it."

He did!

Slim finally admitted that the past several months of stringing me around about the job was nothing more than a reason for him to spend time with me. He admitted that he'd been interested in me from day one. We decided to meet up that evening and talk.

The evening was filled with the deepest and most straight forward conversation we'd ever had together. I let him know that if the relationship was going to work out, I wasn't for the games. I wanted us to work towards something serious. Fuck being a baby momma. I needed to be his only woman, possibly his future wife and I wasn't settling for anything less. Slim agreed. He left me with the sense he was down for the same things. Believing him, I was looking forward to seeing how things would work out between us.

Man, was I in for a reality check.

Being with Slim wasn't at all what I'd expected. Through sources he never revealed, he stalked me, always knowing exactly where I was and who I was with. The shit was creepy. He never wanted to go out, choosing to stay at home and watch television. He also *never* gave me money. I mean not even a single fuckin' penny. Why was it so hard for him to spend a dime on me? Shit, I was honestly beginning to wonder if he was broke. And to add insult to injury...around that same time I happened to be watching Basketball Wives and saw an episode where Ashley Walker and Rafer Skip Alston were on the show together.

Yes, together.

Apparently they had been a couple all along, around the time that he lived in my spot in Harlem. Even when he

was sending me five grand a month.
And when I finally had sex with his ass.
Wow.
Just another time where deceit and lies had entered my life. I learned the hard way that's what happens when you chase athletes and rappers. I was hurt, I can't lie. Not because I wanted to be with him, but because he'd lied to me the entire time. I'd heard of things like that happening to other women, but me....Winter? I took the hit on the chin and moved on.

As time passed, I focused more on Lore'l. She'd started boning this young NY rapper named Jae Millz who was signed to Cash Money. I had actually known him from back in the day. He was cool but as a new artist he had yet to release anything, so his financial situation was nonexistent. Once again, Lore'l was fuckin' for free. Advising her to use him for connections in the game, I decided to just let it go and keep it moving. Besides, I thought it would be kind of cute; possibly like the Big and Lil Kim relationship or the Jay-Z and Foxy thing back in the day. It would help for promotion.

Lore'l quickly fell in love with Jae and began to get side tracked. She started to put more into him than her own career and ignored my advice, which pissed me off. Here I was working my ass off. I felt like I was more interested in her success than she was. Shit, I was even having a difficult time getting her in the studio, which shocked me. The studio was supposed to be an artist's sanctuary, especially a new artist.

Still, despite how hard I tried to give advice on the situation, my words went in one ear and out the other.

Shortly after the two got lovey dovey, the Maybach & Young Money tour started in Orlando. Lore'l flew from NY and I drove in from Miami. After having my mom pick her up from the airport, I met them both at The Amway Arena and called Slim to let him know I was going to be at the show. The last thing I wanted was for him to find out from someone else that I was there, especially if they saw me with Jae Millz. The shit would get super twisted. And I was definitely scared of how he would possibly take it. Being seen around with an up and coming artist could be misunderstood. False conclusions could be drawn. Slim didn't answer so I sent him a text. Still, he didn't respond but I knew he'd gotten the text.

After the concert, I went backstage to use the bathroom and ran dead into Slim. Thank God I was alone. Like I was a groupie, his security swarmed around me. I just laughed and walked right into his arms. The two of us hugged. His tall lanky frame towered over me as the side of my face rested against his chest.

"I called you earlier," I said, still in his arms.

Looking down at me, he said, "I didn't get it."

That was a blatant lie. He was half owner of a multi-million dollar empire. His cell phone was his lifeline. Checking his texts and messages was a must. He was playing games, I knew. He'd probably been hugged up with someone else when my text came through, or maybe he had a chick nearby. I didn't trip though. I'd changed my mentality about men. If he wasn't showing me complete love, I wasn't dishing it out either.

After another hug, I told him I'd hit him up later, knowing most likely we'd spend the night together. Heading to the bathroom, I released a breath I hadn't realized I was holding. My heart was pounding. He truly had me that way. When the show was finally over, against my better judgment, I allowed Lore'l to convince me to ride to the after party on a tour bus. It was a bad idea, a groupie move, but there was no way I was going to leave her alone in that environment.

The party was just what I'd expected. Groupies were all over the place, weed smoke clouded every one, music blared, liquor was guzzled. The bus was so loud I barely heard my phone ring. Seeing Slim's name and number written across the screen, I dipped to the bathroom and closed the door, hoping to alleviate some of the noise. For a moment, I dreaded answering, knowing he was going to be mad. Finally I answered.

"Where you at?" he asked as soon as I pressed the phone to my ear.

"On my way to the after party."

CLICK!

The line went dead, leaving my mouth wide open. Just as I'd known before I got on the bus, it was a bad idea. I knew Slim wasn't going to like it. He wanted me far away from parties, like I was his property. It was always like that with him, which was one thing I hated. It was always his way or no way at all. Despite how I felt, I still attempted to call him back. After he didn't answer, I called his other two numbers but still got no answer. I even sent texts. Nothing worked. Disappointed, I tried to get Lore'l to leave, but she was consumed with Jae Millz. Eventually I cut the night short and spent it at my parents' house.

The next morning, placing that night behind me, I hit Lore'l telling her I would come through to pick her up so we could head back to Miami. It was time to work. I needed to get her in the studio. She didn't answer. After several more calls, she still hadn't answered. Things like this were becoming regular with her. I had to work and was back in Miami when I was finally able to reach her.

When she told me she was going to go with Jae Millz back to Atlanta, I became furious. My sacrifices meant nothing to her. I was hurt. She just wanted to chase dick like a damn air head. Hearing the anger in my voice, she added that she also had to pick up some money from some NFL player. Those words were useless. I suspected she was lying. She wasn't built that way. Getting money out of niggas wasn't how she got down. She was queen of getting pennies out of men. Before I knew it, I slammed the phone down.

I was livid! Cursing like a sailor all over the place. She had no appreciation for what I was trying to do for her and her career. Scotty Boi, a rapper signed to Maybach music at the time, just happened to be available to hear my complaints about Lore'l. He too had been tossing money into my girl's project attempting to make her a sensation. When I told him that Lore'l was trying to follow some rapper to ATL, he lost it. He came over picked me up and drove me to Orlando to get her. On the way up he mentioned getting her into the studio as soon as we got back to Miami.

Unfortunately, once we got to Orlando, there was still no talking sense to her. She didn't quite understand or care about how much had been invested in her. Scotti was so angry, he snapped, "We need to get to work! Fuck chasing a damn nigga!"

Once again, she tried to run that shit about needing to get to Atlanta to get the money from the NFL player. I suspected she was lying. If the player wanted her to have the money, he could send it Western Union or deposit it in her account. The truth was she just wanted to chase Jae Millz like an idiot. I understood the game. I had once been in that arena too. Fortunately, for me, my mindset had changed and I wanted to further myself and my career.

It was becoming obvious I had wasted my time with Lore'l. Giving her the benefit of the doubt, though, I continued to attempt to talk her out of going back to Atlanta. Scotti and I were offering her the chance of a lifetime and we didn't want her to throw it away. Finally, she reluctantly agreed to go back to Miami .

The entire ride back, Lore'l had an attitude. She sat in the back seat damn near pouting like a baby. It was unbelievable. She wouldn't even talk to us. Most aspiring artists would've killed for that opportunity. What made it even worse was that once we reached Miami and tried to get her in the studio, she refused as if punishing me for believing enough in her to want to see her succeed. I couldn't believe her. She really had me wanting to smack her fuckin' hairline back a few inches.

While still in disbelief, Scotti and I both realized that we'd each tried numerous times to get her in the studio and weren't successful. I personally had only seen her in the studio once. It started to occur to me that maybe she wasn't worth my time. Maybe she wasn't really writing her own lyrics and was scared to admit it. That one time I'd seen her in the studio, she was laying a track that was already written. That's when I remembered what Red Café told me...

"She ain't what you think."

No wonder he fell back. The light bulb finally flickered, but I still had love for her and was willing to move past the little episode until I got a call one night while out at dinner.

"Your girl is foul as fuck," a friend of mine said on the other line.

"Who?" I asked, not having any idea who or what he was talking about.

"What did you do to her?"

"I don't even know what you're talking about. *Who* is foul?"

"Lore'l, Winter. She was all up in Wet Willies shittin' on you. She said you let some nigga do something to her."

"What?" I damn near shouted.

My friend went on, saying that Mijiza, my girl from New York, who I had been friends with for over fifteen years, was co-signing the shit. They were together talking about me behind my back like two high school chicks. I couldn't believe it. I knew the incident Lore'l was talking about but it didn't happen how she was saying it did. Mijiza was also there when it happened. She knew Lore'l was lying.

203

How the fuck could she sit there and co-sign I wondered?

The shit sounded so unbelievable that I wasn't quite sure whether to believe it or not. Obviously Lore'l had some bottled up feelings about me since she wasn't returning my calls. Refusing to let it mess up my night, and realizing that she'd just stuck a knife in my back, I silently thought, *we're done*. To this day, I often wonder why Lore'l hasn't made it in her music career. Shit, I wonder if she's actually ever written anything. But what do I know? The girl might be a lyrical genius. She just never showed that side of herself to me. The only thing that continues to aggravate me is the fact that Lore'l never realizes that she fucked up. She owed me from back then. And still does. Still, I always land on my feet.

At that point Roc had to go too. He served no purpose. I got rid of him instantly.

Not long after that incident I hooked up with Ron 'Gutter' Robinson an old friend from my Murder Inc. days. He mentioned that he'd moved to Miami and worked for Flavor Unit Films owned by Queen Latifah and Shakim Compere. We chatted briefly about my current work, who'd I'd recently styled and then he told me Flavor Unit was searching for a Costume Designer for their film department. Just like that I rebounded. That's the beauty in having a resume.

Before I knew it Gutter had hooked up a meeting with one of the heads at Flavor Unit. My resume spoke volumes. I secured the job as Creative Costume Designer. That was just what I needed. A job still in Miami, and with positive people.

Whoever said hard work doesn't pay off lied. My career grew wings and had taken off. Flavor Unit Films began to teach me so much more than what I expected when I was hired. I learned that my styling skills could be sharpened just from being around the right group of people. In addition, being Costume Designer was about more than just picking out clothes—it involved reading scripts and making sure the actors had the right clothing for each scene.

Our work days for filming were consistent—sometimes long. But, at least I knew after the scenes were completed for each day my work hours would end. Just the fact that there was a Monday through Friday schedule excited me. There was no weed smoking, no partying, and no running around the set. Real talk; this was real shit.

Over the course of my first few months I became increasingly nervous. My first movie, "Percentages" was coming up and preparing for my part and responsibilities had me on edge. There were staff meetings, where of course I knew to be on time. Then there were production meetings where we discussed things more specific to our jobs, timing and locations. I wanted to prove to everyone that I could handle the opportunity given to me. I wasn't just cut out for the Hip Hop world.

Eventually production time rolled around. Anxiety filled me. Not necessarily from being around Ving Rhames, Melinda Williams, Cam'ron the rapper, or the other actors in the movie. I'd been around celebs most of my life. My nervousness stemmed from working with Shakim and Otis, another employee of Flavor Unit Films. His team was top notched and expected perfection. Styling artist was more about fashion and making my artist look fly—setting trends. But my new job was more technical—styling for continuity—where my skills were tested. A lot of what I learned had to be self-taught.

By the end of production on "Percentages" I felt like a million bucks. I had come through like I knew I could. In some ways my work would come easy to me. I'd end up working with actors and actresses I admired such as, Omar Gooding, Antwan Tanner, Macy Gray, Clifton Powell, Henry Fonda, Terrance Howard, Jennifer Lewis, Jo Jo Simmons,

Donnell Rawlings, and Alexz Johnson just to name a few. And the pay spoke volumes too. My days of making $300 were over. I now made anywhere from $5,000 to $20,000 per movie, depending on the budget of the movie. Now that made me proud.

Yet more important than money, another positive male was put before me in the form of Shakim Compere. The head honcho around the set, he reminded me of Ted. Married with children, he showed me I didn't have to hang out constantly, smoke and pop bottles to be successful. This man knew how to take care of business the right way and was respected by his entire staff. I admired the way he trusted his team, never micro managing and always making people feel comfortable.

Such a deep, stark contrast to my experiences in Hip Hop. On the surface the two worlds may not have seemed too different. But for me it was as different as night and day.

23 Same Shit, Different Day

Even though I had to drag myself out of bed on the sunniest day Miami had encountered that first week of October 2011, he was still on my mind. The fact that Jason had played me the night before had me wanting to go postal. The mere fact that he'd asked his boy, Bici, to lure me down to Club Play for the Trey Songz video shoot, and then pretended like he didn't know me angered me to the core. His games had gone on for too long. Yet, I found myself pacing the floor, reflecting back on his laugh, his raspy voice, his bald head, the boyish look of his face. All of it turned me on no matter how hard I fought it. For me, Jason was all of the above—a long-time friend and my former lover.

Fuck that! It was war from my view. He knew not to disrespect me in my town. As if he'd known I was thinking about him, Bici texted me once again, this time saying, "Jadakiss said call him." I remember tossing the phone across the room, thinking 'new day, new shit.' Games! There always has to be fuckin' games with him! At first, I wasn't going to respond to the text. Just like he'd shrugged me off last night, like I meant nothing to him, I wanted to dish out

207

the same treatment.

My feelings had gotten to me momentarily. I thought about the night before. I'd pulled up to the club and saw four dudes standing outside, one of them being Jadakiss. I immediately realized I had been set up. Although Bici was one of the men standing outside, Jason was front and center, looking suspicious. Of all the people Bici had said were attending the video shoot, he'd failed to mention Jason. He'd informed me that Fab was inside so chatting it up with him would be cool, so I stayed after hugging Bici tightly, along with two other dudes from my past, Groovy Lew and Ice Pick. They both complimented me on what I was wearing, but of course not Jason. Like clockwork, he paid me no mind. He gave me a few glances but that was it. No words, no compliments, no conversation. Nothing. Yet, all in all, it was revealed that Jadakiss was the one who wanted me to come to the club. I waved him off and headed inside to chat with Fab.

When my phone sounded again, I looked back at the text, hoping to forget the night before. I couldn't help myself. I wanted to hear what my cocky, shady friend had to say.

"What's up?" I said dryly the moment he answered.

"I'm sorry 'bout last night," he said softly.

I rolled my eyes. "Jason, you owe me breakfast, lunch and dinner for the shit you pulled last night. Why you always acting like you not feeling me?"

"Just come through, I got you," he said nonchalantly. "Nore's shooting a movie today."

"Bet, I'm on the way."

Since I considered myself Slim's woman, I knew he wouldn't like the idea of me hanging out with a notable rapper like Jadakiss, I figured he wouldn't find out. Although they both were in the industry, Slim was on a different level; a caliber most couldn't touch. He kept his world quiet and classy, so I figured their worlds wouldn't clash. Besides, I couldn't resist seeing Jason while he was in my town, and it seemed like the perfect opportunity to network, maybe a job would come out of it somehow. People who knew me well understood that I was always looking for another way to make money. Before I knew it, I agreed to go see him.

A couple of hours later, I found myself walking in the door of his suite. There were about a dozen people already there which surprised me. I'd assumed we were going to be alone, but then again, it worked to my advantage. As usual, weed smoke was loud as I was greeted by several of the people in the room, each showing me love. Most of them had been at the video shoot the previous night. Music was playing and liquor was being guzzled. Unlike last night, Jason actually acknowledged me. He greeted me with a pound like I was one of his homies rather than giving me a hug or a kiss. That irked me but at least he spoke this time.

It didn't take long for the room to clear. It seemed as if everyone peeled out within seconds. When it finally emptied, I snapped on Jason. "Jason, tell me why you had Bici text me last night and then you acted like I didn't exist? We've been friends for too long."

"What do you mean?"

"Look, don't play stupid! You know what I mean! You always do this shit! You've been doing it for years now. It's called being fake!"

He shook his head like I was stressing him. "I see you the same old Winter. Still Hollywood."

"I'm tired of going through this with you, Jason!"

He looked me in the eyes and said, "Hollywood, you know how I feel about you. I just don't like the whole world in my business."

"So, you ignore me in front of everyone?"

"I apologize for that."

His apology did nothing to ease my frustration. "I can't

tell. I think you're letting this stardom shit go to your head."

"Go 'head with that. So what you been up to?"

"I've been working at Flavor unit," I told him proudly, mad that he'd changed the subject. I paused, unsure of how much of my business to really share with him. I looked at him standing there with a sense of entitlement because of our history together, the same history that seemed to mean nothing to him anymore. I hoped that he didn't think that just because we'd been lovers in the past, he was entitled to some ass from me since we were alone. Even though I'd messed with plenty of well-knowns in the industry, I wasn't a jump off. That wasn't me. We took it easy and reminisced a bit until things lightened up.

Soon, I decided to confide in him about my new business opportunity. I told him Mona Scott-Young was considering creating Love & Hip Hop of Miami and that she wanted me on the show. Love & Hip Hop is a successful reality show that launched on VH1 and focuses on the lives of women in the Hip Hop world. It originated in New York and spun off to Atlanta. Miami would be the latest franchise.

"What's your thoughts on it?" I asked. Honestly, I'd thought he wouldn't agree with it but he surprised me. He seemed more excited about it than me.

"Are you serious? Yo, you should do it," he said. "This is your time to shine! Whatever you need from me, I got you!"

He seemed totally supportive and I loved it. Jason could always motivate me. When we were together sexually, I was inspired by his motivation and determination to succeed. I loved that part of him, but still had those mixed feelings lingering. He was like a see-saw. The man I knew so well had a warm side, but others knew him as this hard, Hip Hop sensation. Now he had me feeling good about him and *us* once again. Just the thought of how things could be for our friendship from this point excited me. I needed someone experienced in the business to coach me in the Reality TV world. He would be perfect.

"Yo, Hollywood, fa real, this gon' be hot! You gon' be a star!"

I smiled, thankful for his support. It really did mean a lot to me.

"So I can depend on you to mentor me about the business?"

"Didn't I say I got you?"

At that point I truly believed him. I trusted him. As I listened to him talk, my heart softened more and more. I was reminded of the man he used to be. I was reminded of how great things were between us when I was in college and his dream of being a huge rapper was coming true. Things truly were different then.

"I really want things to go back the way they were, Hollywood, but as friends. I fucked up and I realize that. I had a good thing with you. Can we at least try?"

A part of me wanted so desperately to believe him. His words sounded genuine and honest, but there was the issue of Slim. He was my $350 million dollar man and was my main priority. Was Kiss now trying to insert himself back into the picture? Was Jason trying to be more than a friend? He now looked and sounded just like the man I'd grown up with.

"You know you gon' need a boyfriend on the show right?"

That comment threw me off completely. At that point, his motives weren't clear to me. Crazy thoughts flooded my mind. I thought of Slim. If he knew I was in Jadakiss' hotel room he'd spaz on me, but having Jason go on the show with me as my boyfriend was out of the question. Did Jason need the show just as much as I did?

Jason's career had skidded over the years. His records weren't selling like they'd been when he first came into the game, but he still had that same cocky swagger with which he'd entered the game. That still turned me on about him. Still, another part of me, the rational side, made sure to remind me of the games he'd been playing. It reminded me of all the times he said one thing on the phone but turned around and did something else in public. I could see us on the show together and then he'd back out at the last minute.

"Jason, how do I know you're serious?"

"Because I am. I know I haven't given you reason to trust me but it is the truth. I wouldn't lie about something this serious. I still want you in my life as a friend. I really need more people around me I can trust."

I saw something in him I hadn't seen in years. It touched me. He sounded and looked too real for me not to believe him. In my heart, I really felt he was telling the truth. I could feel in my soul that he wanted to do right by our friendship.

"I don't know. I may not do the show," I abruptly told him.

"Are you crazy?" he said. "This is a hell of an opportunity. Once you're on the show, the whole world will open up for you. People will know your name and face. You'll be able to step off into fashion, hosting opportunities and a whole lot of shit. And you need to write a book. Yo, Hollywood, you can't pass this up. This is an opportunity people kill for."

Jason definitely made sense. He'd been in the industry for over fifteen years so he had experience. He knew what he was talking about and with him by my side guiding me, I could go further than I would on my own. Besides, the book thing sounded great since I had written in my journal since the Fabolous days. For the rest of the night, we talked mainly about the show. Hours flew by and it was time for me to leave. The two of us agreed to stay in touch and he promised to call the following day.

The next morning rolled around with Jason reverting right back to his old self—full of shit. You know you're truly feeling someone if you check *their social media* before you check your own. I got on my computer and went to his twitter page, wishing I could lose the feelings I had for him. What I did next was considered stalking. His page was filled with recent posts and photos of him while in Miami. Nearly every picture had bitches in them. It was like I had a front row seat, watching him and his friends popping bottles and trickin' on every chick in the photos. Jealousy invaded my veins. I hated feeling that way, especially for a screw-up who didn't feel that same way about me, but that's what you got when you mess around with Platinum record selling artists who smell themselves too much.

Why couldn't I let go of my feelings for him? Why did I care about who he was with? I had someone I was interested in and who cared about me. Why should I have cared how many women he was trickin'?

Eventually, I put all emotions aside, this was business. I needed him, and he needed me.

After that night, we began to talk more often. I never told him how angry I was for not being invited out with him while he was still in Miami. Besides, he really seemed to be trying to change. All the things he'd said while in Miami seemed to have been the truth. He was definitely putting forth a commendable effort.

When November 2011 came, I ended up in New York and on the Love and Hip Hop set to tape my cameo giving Emily advice about Fab. Sadly, all deals were off for the Miami show, but there were some talks of me coming on Season 3, NewYork as a cast member. So many thoughts flooded my mind: Would that show be a good look for me? Would I have to come in contact with my old flings? I wasn't really sure if the opportunity was right for me. I needed guidance.

Thankfully, Slim was in Australia and even though we'd talked on the phone countless times, he had no idea I had done the episode. He wouldn't have gone for it. Yet Jason was right there. As soon as I got off set, Jason asked me to meet up with him. The two of us wound up spending a night together at his place. We just chilled, no sex. We spent that entire night talking mainly about the advice I'd given Emily and if I was ready to step into the big leagues. Jason still seemed more excited about the show than me. He gave me tons of advice and helped me plan for it. All of the advice and encouragement continued over the next four or five months. I'd kept Jason in the loop about *everything* involving the show, including my pay rate, my talks with VH1 executives and show producers and also my talks with Viacom. I'd even confided in him personal secrets about my life no one else knew. I trusted him that much. He'd truly grown to become my confidant and I knew I could trust him.

Or at least I thought I could.

A few weeks later I was back in Miami when I got the call from the Love and Hip Hop show. I rushed back to New York to finally sign my deal as a new cast member. I called Jason for some last minute advice. Everything seemed cool. During the conversation, he reminded me that my appearance on the show would be hotter if I let him come on as my boyfriend as Jadakiss. Obviously, since I was with Slim, that couldn't happen. I had to tell him, "no." By the time the conversation was over, I honestly thought he understood. I thought there were no hard feelings, but I couldn't have been more wrong.

There are two things I can't stand: when somebody tries to play me for slow and when people, especially those who are *supposed* to be *good people*, use me.

That irks the shit out of me.

That rejection had obviously hit a nerve. The next time I called Jason, he didn't answer. I called him several more times but still got no answer. Before long, two days had passed. He still wasn't answering his phone or returning my texts or messages. At first, I tried to give him the benefit of the doubt. Maybe he'd lost his phone or it had been stolen. Maybe he was busy. Maybe. Maybe. Maybe. Eventually I had to come out of denial. It broke my heart but I had to realize...

I'd been played...by someone I thought was a true friend.

I still loved Jason. He still had my heart. I couldn't deny it but he'd played me for the last time. My tolerance level for users dropped extremely low at that point. I could only take so much.

Out of nowhere, Jason finally texted me back.

DON'T SIGN.

I called him immediately to find out why he didn't want me to sign. Did he know something I didn't know? Was something going to happen on the show I wasn't prepared for? I had a million questions but he didn't answer. I sent him several texts but he still didn't respond.

Before that text, I'd listened carefully to all his advice. I had valued it. I didn't think he would steer me wrong. He'd seemed so pro-Hollywood, so sincere about us getting our friendship back on track, so happy about seeing me succeed. Yet now, just like he'd done before, he switched up on me and broke my heart. Now he didn't even care enough to even give me a damn call. Then it hit me. There was that one thing that hurt me above all...

He'd tried to *use* me! My guess, if I'd agreed to have him on the show as my boyfriend, things would have been different. Rapper or not, he could now, kiss my ass!

We all know skills don't pay the bills. A new generation of Hip Hop fans has risen and their money goes towards what's hot, and what we see plastered over the TV. The best way to become relevant again, he probably felt, was to come on Love & Hip Hop with me. That's the only way I can explain how he played me.

The realization pissed me off, but rather than let it eat me up, something Jason had said played inside of my head...

"It's your time to shine, Hollywood!"

He was right. In the midst of a sad situation, I decided to take something good from it. I realized and accepted that I had to stand on my own and do what was best for me. Against Jason's advice, I signed my deal as a cast member of Love & Hip Hop Season 3. Someday I'll thank him for putting that battery in my back.

During that whole ordeal, I never told Slim about the episode I'd done with Emily. Everything happened so quickly, I was back in Miami before he even noticed. He'd been in Australia for a week or so which gave me time to do me. As the two of us continued to get to know each other, besides his sources stalking me and his unwillingness to spend any money on me, I also discovered how childish he was. That came out on New Year's Eve 2011. His brother Birdman was hosting a Cash Money NYE party. As usual, Slim didn't come out. Something about the attention, bright lights and crowds never sat well with him. He just didn't like the spotlight at all. Anyway, I was enjoying myself that night just like everyone else at the party when my cell rang. The festivities were so loud that I couldn't really hear him through the phone. With a finger plugged into my left ear in an attempt to hear him, I had to ask him to repeat himself a few times. Evidently he didn't like that at all. He hung up. He then sent a text.

I'm not coming if you're looking for me.

I wasn't surprised. I hadn't expected him to show up. But I wasn't going to spend my New Year's Eve cooped up in the damn house. Still wanting to see him before the night was over, though, I sent him a text asking if he wanted to see me. Instead of saying yes or no, he simply returned a text telling me to enjoy myself and don't stay out too late.

Games! Fuckin' games!

He was mad at me for not devoting my *entire* night to him. It was always that way with him. He wanted me to come over. But instead of admitting it, he'd rather act like a damn child and pout about it. From that night on, we were in and out of touch.

As I said before, being with Slim wasn't what I'd expected at all. To add to the strangeness, we never fucked. That scared me. It made me honestly wonder why? I wasn't sure. Things between me and him began to grow shaky, finally ending in an eruption the night my episode of Love & Hip Hop New York Season 2 aired. He'd told me he hadn't seen it but at eleven o'clock that night he called and asked me to come over. I did. Within just several minutes, I was pulling up to the building his penthouse was located in. After passing my keys to the valet, I hopped the elevator. As soon as I stepped off the elevator and walked into the private elevator entrance of his penthouse, he snapped.

"Why the fuck you do something like that without telling me?" he shouted like he was my father.

I was totally caught by surprise. He'd never spoken to me like that before. He'd never raised his voice. Also, I had no idea what he was talking about.

"What are you talking about?" I asked.

"Don't play dumb! I'm talking about the damn show!"

He'd told me earlier he hadn't seen it.

"You wanna be on TV, huh? You just like the rest of these women! You ain't nothing but a groupie!"

He was furious. The look in his eyes said he wanted to slap me.

"It's not like that," I attempted. "I kind of did it for Fab. He didn't have anyone to speak up for him."

"Oh, so you did fuck Fab?"

That was just his way of fishing for information. He

was always inquiring about who I'd fucked in the industry. I felt like he was too insecure. I'd told him before that I hadn't fucked Fab but I knew he didn't believe me.

"No, I didn't fuck him." I returned.

"Then why else would you want to protect him?!"

"Slim, it's not what you think. We're just friends. Look, I know people in this industry and you can't change that. Stop assuming that I fucked everyone I know in this industry. Some are just friends and business associates, that's all. I've worked in the industry longer than you. I just haven't been as successful."

By the look on his face, he wasn't buying it, although it really was the truth. I tried to plead my case but he didn't want anything else to do with me. As far as he was concerned, I'd made him look stupid by appearing on the show. He was afraid people would draw the same misconception about my and Fab's relationship that he did. And the last thing he wanted the public to think or know was that a rapper had fucked his woman. He'd worked too hard to build his empire and didn't want this to jeopardize it. But more so, his anger was out of pride and ego.

"Slim," I tried.

"Get out!"

Realizing there was nothing more I could say to convince him I was sorry, I grabbed my purse and left, saddened that it was probably over between us. Definitely needing a drink, I headed straight to The King of Diamonds. As I ran through several shots of Patron and reminisced on the moments Slim and I had shared together, I forced myself to accept that the relationship was over.

Maybe a missed opportunity for me?

Maybe not.

24   Still Standing

2012 came bursting in with a bang and the worry of men had evaporated from my heart. Between my gig at Flavor Unit Films and officially filming season three of Love &Hip Hop, I was staying busy. Maintaining good working relationships had paid off. Through the positive connections I had made I'd gotten calls to style Meek Mills, Wale and Trey Songz, for the Video, "Face Down". I had also styled R&B singer Tank and fellow Love & Hip Hop cast member, Tahiry for the "Love Like This" video featuring rapper MSG. Tank was on the hook and Tahiry the girl in the video. I'd even styled Knick's point guard, J.R Smith for some needed promo materials. But nothing compared to getting the last minute phone call where a stylist was needed for Nicki Minaj for "The Today Show."

Dreams really do come true. It's strange when I look back on a lot of my introductions to celebrities. Just like with Skip and Swizz, most of them just happened. I hadn't planned them. They just fell right into my lap without me even trying. I guess somebody upstairs really likes me.

I'd like to think I created a success story out of what could've been a disaster. I'd like to think I've grown. There are so many things I could've done differently, some I'm not so proud of…but that's life. You live…you learn.

My work ethics now make me smile and I'm most proud of the working relationships I've built. Just from knowing Benzino, owner of *Hip Hop Weekly* from the Murder Inc. days, allowed me to call him after the controversial advice I gave Emily on Love & Hip Hop Season 2. I thought it would bring a good spark to the magazine if I was able to give other females advice on how to handle men. He agreed, and soon my column, Ask Winter appeared in *Hip Hop Weekly*. I'm still writing that column today.

Through the column, I let women know that the hip hop world may seem like a stunning and amazing place to be swept up in, but there's a price to pay if you want to be a part of it. The fascination behind the lives of rappers, athletes, celebs and ballers is hard to shake, especially now with so much media focus. But trust and believe maintaining a relationship with one of these guys has never been, and will never be easy. You have to know what you are getting yourself into, what you want out of the relationship, and what you're willing to put up with.

As I've said before, I have seen the dark side of this Hip Hop game; the brutality and domestic violence. And I wouldn't wish some of it on my worst enemy.

Journal Entry

I never thought I would have to experience this ever. The first black eye I was told was an accident. But now he's comfortable enough to do this in front of all of us. Is he on drugs? I didn't think he had it in him. The dragging down the stairs and violent behavior made me look at him different. I wanted to team up with her and kick his ass but after the fight she acted like it was ok that it happened. I'm totally confused now. I've never had to deal with this. Obviously this is something she was used to. Did she get roughed up like this before? I always said if it happens with other men then maybe she did something to deserve it... But fuck that nobody deserves to be hurt that way. No bag. shoes, car or anything else is worth feeling the pain I heard in her screams. I'm sure I'll have nightmares after this. Bitch ass nigga scared in the street but can do this to his girl in front of her kid. Fucking punk.

I need to tell someone who can help but who. He doesn't listen to anyone. There's a child in here and these niggas walking around here saying we may have to bury her in the backyard one day. How can I stand by and allow this to happen. I wasn't comfortable enough to talk to him about it but I was stupid to think the first black eye was an accident. Maybe his manager would be able to get to him. We didn't need her really getting hurt or even calling the cops. I'm not sure if there are guns or drugs in here and this is the last thing he needed for his career and reputation. His boys thought it was funny but I swear I cry myself to sleep at night trying to figure out how to help.

Journal Entry

I got up enough courage today to talk to her about what's going on. She admitted it happened in a previous relationship. And even gave specific details of incidents in the past. The way she spoke was like she was used to it and didn't really mind. I decided that now I need to mind my business. You are content with what's going on so why am I losing sleep over it. Obviously the material things and the good times outweigh the ass whippings. I'll just mind my business and go downstairs the next time something like this happens. And I'm sure there are more ass whippings in the future. This Hip Hop shit is out of control.

Some of the same women I've seen get abused, most assume are living the good life just because they're on television or dating a celebrity. These same women can't even get someone to stop the abuse because they don't want to confront a rapper or celeb. Although I never got pulled down a staircase my ups and downs in the industry run a close match. I guess these experiences—good and bad had to happen to make me the person I am today. I now have the confidence to understand, I don't need a certain type of man to validate me. I don't have to be with a rapper, athlete, or someone with money. I still have my faith and have come to grips with waiting for the right man as the best solution rather than trying out every man.

No more games.

I truly believe every man was brought into my life for a reason and served their purpose. There were many lessons learned from each of them. The personality traits of men I've slept with have rubbed off on me in some way, most likely remaining with me for the rest of my life. Of course there are some who I assume never had an orgasm since I see none of their characteristics in myself.

I believe I picked up my business sense from Dame and Swizz, absorbing some of their intelligence cells and my young energetic, spirit from Young Berg. I'm known to have the mouth of a squawking bird, loud and over the top at times. Surely that came from Slim Thug. Add that to my ability to stand up for myself and demand what I want, which no doubt came from Smiley. Of course every time I find myself in a brawl, I think of Skip—hot head.

Jadakiss and Big Money possess so many of the same traits it's hard to tell where each contributed, yet through them both certainly I gained determination, power and selfishness all at the same time. They knew how to hustle and grind—hard. They each had the will power to never give up, something that sticks with me today.

Just like your spouse can mess up your credit, or your lover can make you smile, there's the good and bad you take from every relationship. At times I was drawn to these guys just for money, sometimes it was just sex. Then there were times when it wasn't either. These men all represented all the best aspects of what I expected out of life at the time; fun, travel, excitement, love, sex, grinding, passion, and hustle.

I hold no grudges against any of them. They handled me the best way they knew how.

No retaliation needed. I'm still on top. I have my sanity, my friends, my family, my faith, and now a host of readers to lean on.

I really have grown up.

Game Over.

For More Book Titles Please Visit

www.lifechangingbooks.net

facebook.com/lifechangingbooks
Twitter: @lcbooks
Instagram:@lcbbooks

ORDER FORM

MAIL TO:
PO Box 423
Brandywine, MD 20613
301-362-6508

Ship to:	
Address:	
City & State:	Zip:

Date:	Phone:
Email:	

Make all money orders and cashiers checks payable to: **Life Changing Books**

Qty.	ISBN	Title	Release Date	Price
	0-9741394-2-4	Bruised by Azarel	Jul-05	$ 15.00
	0-9741394-7-5	Bruised 2: The Ultimate Revenge by Azarel	Oct-06	$ 15.00
	0-9741394-3-2	Secrets of a Housewife by J. Tremble	Feb-06	$ 15.00
	0-9741394-6-7	The Millionaire Mistress by Tiphani	Nov-06	$ 15.00
	1-934230-99-5	More Secrets More Lies by J. Tremble	Feb-07	$ 15.00
	1-934230-95-2	A Private Affair by Mike Warren	May-07	$ 15.00
	1-934230-96-0	Flexin & Sexin Volume 1	Jun-07	$ 15.00
	1-934230-89-8	Still a Mistress by Tiphani	Nov-07	$ 15.00
	1-934230-91-X	Daddy's House by Azarel	Nov-07	$ 15.00
	1-934230-88-X	Naughty Little Angel by J. Tremble	Feb-08	$ 15.00
	1-934230820	Rich Girls by Kendall Banks	Oct-08	$ 15.00
	1-934230839	Expensive Taste by Tiphani	Nov-08	$ 15.00
	1-934230782	Brooklyn Brothel by C. Stecko	Jan-09	$ 15.00
	1-934230669	Good Girl Gone bad by Danette Majette	Mar-09	$ 15.00
	1-934230804	From Hood to Hollywood by Sasha Raye	Mar-09	$ 15.00
	1-934230707	Sweet Swagger by Mike Warren	Jun-09	$ 15.00
	1-934230677	Carbon Copy by Azarel	Jul-09	$ 15.00
	1-934230723	Millionaire Mistress 3 by Tiphani	Nov-09	$ 15.00
	1-934230715	A Woman Scorned by Ericka Williams	Nov-09	$ 15.00
	1-934230685	My Man Her Son by J. Tremble	Feb-10	$ 15.00
	1-924230731	Love Heist by Jackie D.	Mar-10	$ 15.00
	1-934230812	Flexin & Sexin Volume 2	Apr-10	$ 15.00
	1-934230748	The Dirty Divorce by Miss KP	May-10	$ 15.00
	1-934230758	Chedda Boyz by CJ Hudson	Jul-10	$ 15.00
	1-934230766	Snitch by VegasClarke	Oct-10	$ 15.00
	1-934230693	Money Maker by Tonya Ridley	Oct-10	$ 15.00
	1-934230774	The Dirty Divorce Part 2 by Miss KP	Nov-10	$ 15.00
	1-934230170	The Available Wife by Carla Pennington	Jan-11	$ 15.00
	1-934230774	One Night Stand by Kendall Banks	Feb-11	$ 15.00
	1-934230278	Bitter by Danette Majette	Feb-11	$ 15.00
	1-934230299	Married to a Balla by Jackie D.	May-11	$ 15.00
	1-934230308	The Dirty Divorce Part 3 by Miss KP	Jun-11	$ 15.00
	1-934230316	Next Door Nympho By CJ Hudson	Jun-11	$ 15.00
	1-934230286	Bedroom Gangsta by J. Tremble	Sep-11	$ 15.00
	1-934230340	Another One Night Stand by Kendall Banks	Oct-11	$ 15.00
	1-934230359	The Available Wife Part 2 by Carla Pennington	Nov-11	$ 15.00
	1-934230332	Wealthy & Wicked by Chris Renee	Jan-12	$ 15.00
	1-934230375	Life After a Balla by Jackie D.	Mar-12	$ 15.00
	1-934230251	V.I.P. by Azarel	Apr-12	$ 15.00
	1-934230383	Welfare Grind by Kendall Banks	May-12	$ 15.00
	1-934230413	Still Grindin' by Kendall Banks	Sep-12	$ 15.00
	1-934230391	Paparazzi by Miss KP	Oct-13	$ 15.00
	1-93423043X	Cashin' Out by Jai Nicole	Nov-12	$ 15.00
	1-934230634	Welfare Grind Part 3 by Kendall Banks	Mar-13	$15.00
	1-934230642	Game Over by Winter Ramos	Apr-13	$15.99
			Total for Books	$

* Prison Orders- Please allow up to three (3) weeks for delivery.	Shipping Charges (add $4.95 for 1-4 books*)	$
	Total Enclosed (add lines)	$

Please Note: We are not held responsible for returned prison orders. Make sure the facility will receive books before ordering.

*Shipping and Handling of 5-10 books is $6.95, please contact us if your order is more than 10 books. (301)362-6508